Issues in Testing: Coaching, Disclosure, and Ethnic Bias

Bert F. Green, *Editor*

NEW DIRECTIONS FOR TESTING AND MEASUREMENT
WILLIAM B. SCHRADER, *Editor-in-Chief*

Number 11, September 1981

Paperback sourcebooks in
The Jossey-Bass Social and Behavioral Sciences Series

Jossey-Bass Inc., Publishers
San Francisco • Washington • London

Issues in Testing: Coaching, Disclosure, and Ethnic Bias
Number 11, September 1981
    Bert F. Green, *Editor*

New Directions for Testing and Measurement Series
William B. Schrader, *Editor-in-Chief*

New Directions for Testing and Measurement is published
quarterly by Jossey-Bass Inc., Publishers. Subscriptions, single-issue
orders, change of address notices, undelivered copies, and other
correspondence should be sent to *New Directions* Subscriptions,
Jossey-Bass Inc., Publishers, 433 California Street, San Francisco,
California 94104.

Editorial correspondence should be sent to the Editor-in-Chief,
William B. Schrader, ETS, Princeton, New Jersey 08541.

Library of Congress Catalogue Card Number LC 80-85264
International Standard Serial Number ISSN 0271-0609
International Standard Book Number ISBN 87589-873-4

Cover art by Willi Baum
Manufactured in the United States of America

Ordering Information

The paperback sourcebooks listed below are published quarterly and can be ordered either by subscription or as single copies.

Subscriptions cost $30.00 per year for institutions, agencies, and libraries. Individuals can subscribe at the special rate of $18.00 per year *if payment is by personal check.* (Note that the full rate of $30.00 applies if payment is by institutional check, even if the subscription is designated for an individual.) Standing orders are accepted.

Single copies are available at $6.95 when payment accompanies order, and *all single-copy orders under $25.00 must include payment.* (California, Washington, D.C., New Jersey, and New York residents please include appropriate sales tax.) For billed orders, cost per copy is $6.95 plus postage and handling. (Prices subject to change without notice.)

To ensure correct and prompt delivery, all orders must give either the *name of an individual* or an *official purchase order number.* Please submit your order as follows:

Subscriptions: specify series and subscription year.
Single Copies: specify sourcebook code and issue number (such as, TM8).

Mail orders for United States and Possessions, Latin America, Canada, Japan, Australia, and New Zealand to:
Jossey-Bass Inc., Publishers
433 California Street
San Francisco, California 94104

Mail orders for all other parts of the world to:
Jossey-Bass Limited
28 Banner Street
London EC1Y 8QE

New Directions for Testing and Measurement Series
William B. Schrader, *Editor-in-Chief*

Contents

Editor's Notes

Standardized tests are widely used in personnel selection processes in industry, and in selecting student applicants to colleges and universities. In recent years, these tests have been severely criticized by several groups for various perceived or suspected flaws. In particular, academic selection tests have been criticized for being secret, biased, and susceptible to coaching.

The main reason for the use of admission tests is to have a common yardstick for all applicants. Applicants come from different schools with different grading practices, so the previous educational accomplishments of the various applicants cannot easily be compared. The intent of the test is to give everyone a fair and equitable chance, whatever their background and whatever their charisma.

But are tests really fair? Is it fair if some students can improve their scores by spending several hundred dollars to attend a coaching school? Is it fair if poor students, or black students, have less chance to obtain the general background needed to do well on the tests? Is it fair if the tests are kept secret so that no one can check on the accuracy of the scores, the accuracy of the keyed answers, or the nature of the items?

Because tests are important in the lives of students and job applicants, testing practices deserve public scrutiny. The issues must be aired in all their complexities so that the informed citizen can form an intelligent opinion. This sourcebook is a step toward that goal.

Aptitudes and abilities are often viewed as fixed, inherent traits of an individual that are essentially unmodifiable by experience. If so, measures of these traits should also be fixed, except for random measurement error, and should not be affected by short-term coaching or by any form of special preparation. If test scores can be affected by coaching, then there would seem to be something wrong with the test. Anne Anastasi considers this general problem by first examining what is being measured, and, second, what is meant by coaching. She discusses the nature of aptitude and intelligence tests and what they measure. This sage analysis provides a clear perspective for discussions of many testing problems, including coaching. When we further understand that special preparation for the test can mean anything from extensive education to intensive practice in test-taking, we begin to see the wider dimensions of the coaching problem.

Samuel Messick then gives a detailed analysis of the specific problem of coaching effects on the College Entrance Examination Board's

Scholastic Aptitude Test (SAT). Well-established coaching schools will, for a substantial tuition fee, provide instruction on test-taking strategies and extensive drill in taking tests equivalent to the target test. To the extent that coaching helps, students who can afford the time and money to obtain coaching will gain an unfair advantage. If coaching does not help, the claims of the coaching schools are fraudulent and their patrons are being bilked. Messick analyzes the pertinent data and considers the many implications of his conclusions.

Although the coaching issue is important, short-term coaching effects are relatively small. By contrast, ethnic differences are large. On the average, blacks score much lower than whites on most aptitude and ability tests. This actuarial statement about averages should not be misunderstood. Some black students earn the highest possible score, and some white students earn the lowest possible score. Indeed, every possible score is earned by some students of each group. But, as a group, the scores of black students are lower than the scores of white students. Similar, but less-striking differences are found for other ethnic groups. Are these differences real or merely an artifact of the tests? There are two major aspects of this question. A test as a whole might be biased, or the tests might contain some items that are biased. Lloyd Bond focuses on the general question of test bias, and Lorrie Shepard emphasizes item bias. (Multiple-choice test "questions" are nearly always declarative sentences so the syntactically neutral term, "item," is preferred to "question.") Neither item bias nor test bias is a straight-forward issue. There are many definitions of bias, each with an implied method for detecting bias in any particular instance. The issues are complex and require careful, clear thought.

Even if tests, or some items on tests, turn out to be biased, the extent of the bias is not likely to be large enough to explain most, or even a large part, of the observed group difference. The difference is too profound. It is legitimate to question test bias, but it is also legitimate to view the test as a social indicator. The American ideal is that every person should have an equal chance to develop his or her potential to the fullest. Whatever the results on test bias, the tests also serve to indicate that the ideal is a long way from being realized.

Concerns about coachability and bias are part of a general tendency to be wary of any secret enterprise. Test critics have led a recent clamor for open testing. They want that the actual items on a test, and their correct answers, to be published after the test has been administered. Currently, New York is the only state with a law requiring open testing, but similar bills have been introduced in many state legislatures and in the U.S. Congress. Open testing has several intended effects. The test-taker can check that the correct answers were indeed correct, and that his or her answer sheet was scored correctly. Also the test items can be inspected for possible bias.

Test disclosure has some adverse effects. A test cannot be reused so a new test would be necessary for every open administration of the test. This means that a great many more test items would be needed. Test items are not easy to write; further, every test item must be pretested before it is actually used on a test. Thus, the cost of test construction would rise dramatically and quality might be threatened. If each test administration requires a new test, special provisions could no longer be made for persons whose religious convictions preclude their taking the test on the regularly scheduled day, or students who were just too late to register for the test but badly need a timely test score. Special test forms for the handicapped (cassette, Braille, and so on) would not be economically feasible.

Gary Marco discusses one further serious statistical problem that arises; one that is seldom recognized. In open testing, it is extremely difficult to ensure comparability of test scores across test forms. The SAT and other ongoing test programs use many different, equivalent forms of the test. Several new forms are constructed every year, each with different items. Since each test is to some extent unique, it cannot be expected that a given person will get the same raw score on every form of the test. Apart from random measurement errors, some forms might be slightly easier than other forms. Moreover, the groups of people who take the test on each test administration cannot be assumed to be equally able; therefore, each test cannot simply be standardized to a fixed mean and standard deviation for the group taking that test form. Rather, the scaled scores on the various test forms must be adjusted or *equated* so that any given scaled score represents the same level of ability. Unless the test forms are carefully equated, a person's score could depend, in part, on which test form he took or on when he took the test.

The process of test equating is not widely understood, even by measurement specialists. Marco describes the process, points out the extra difficulties that are raised by test disclosure, and tells what steps can be taken to equate tests that must be disclosed. Advocates of open testing claim that equating is a technical matter that can be repaired by psychometricians. As it turns out, this confidence was not misplaced, but the problem is still acute, still under study, and worthy of public attention.

Bert F. Green
Editor

Bert F. Green, who is professor of psychology at The Johns Hopkins University, has recently chaired the research committee of the Graduate Record Examinations Board, and has just finished an eight-year term as editor of Psychometrika.

The essential question is not how far test scores can be improved by special training programs, but how such improvement relates to cognitive behavior in real-life contexts.

Diverse Effects of Training on Tests of Academic Intelligence

Anne Anastasi

Popular discussions of the effects of coaching on test performance have been concerned chiefly with tests of "scholastic aptitude" or "general intelligence." Much controversy on this topic arises in part from ambiguity and lack of uniformity in the use of terms. To clear away some of the prevalent confusion, we shall examine first the nature of the tests involved in this controversy. Then we shall consider coaching against the background of diverse types of training that may affect test performance, and we shall inquire into the implications of these various forms of training for the meaning and validity of test scores.

What Do Intelligence Tests Measure?

The late 1970s witnessed a resurgence of interest in the concept of intelligence. This revival of interest does not imply a return to former

This chapter is based in part on invited addresses given in May 1980 at the Connecticut State Psychological Association and at the School of Psychology, Georgia Institute of Technology.

B. F. Green (Ed.), *New Directions for Testing and Measurement: Issues in Testing—Coaching, Disclosure, and Ethnic Bias,* no. 11. San Francisco: Jossey-Bass, September 1981.

views about the nature of intelligence. The concept that is now emerging differs in several important ways from the earlier concept of intelligence that prevailed from the turn of the century to the 1930s, and that still survives in popular discussions of intelligence, intelligence testing, and that particular horror, the IQ. It is well to remember that the IQ was never meant to refer to a trait of the organism, nor to a kind of test. It was only a kind of score—and a poor kind of score at that. In fact, as a score it has been largely replaced by standard scores, as in the so-called deviation IQ of the Wechsler scales and the Stanford-Binet, among others.

This crude, distorted notion of intelligence is *not* what I see revivified in the 1980s. Rather, a new concept of intelligence is emerging among a group of psychometricians who are also knowledgeable in psychology. It is a sophisticated and technically refined concept that reflects the accumulated store of relevant research findings from various disciplines. This concept of intelligence is characterized by explicit definition and by the deletion of excess meanings, vague assumptions, and fuzzy implications. When freed from these encrustations, intelligence tests are seen as measures of what the individual has learned to do and what he or she knows at the time. Tests can serve a predictive function only insofar as they indicate to what extent the individual has acquired the prerequisite skills and knowledge for a designated criterion performance. What persons can accomplish in the future depends not only on their present intellectual status, as assessed by the test, but also on their subsequent experiences.

Furthermore, intelligence tests are descriptive, not explanatory. No intelligence test can indicate the reason for one's performance. To attribute inadequate performance on a test or in everyday-life activities to "inadequate intelligence" is a tautology and in no way advances our understanding of the individual's handicap. In fact, it may halt efforts to explore the causes of the handicap in the individual's experiential history. Intelligence tests should be used, not to label individuals but to assess their current status. To bring persons to their maximum functioning level we need to start where they are at the time; we need to identify their strengths and weaknesses and plan accordingly.

Having scraped off the excess, implied meanings, we can recognize that intelligence tests measure a limited but important domain of cognitive skills and knowledge. To help us understand more specifically what these tests actually measure, there is available a vast accumulation of data, derived from both clinical observations and hundreds of validity studies against academic and occupational criteria. The findings indicate that the particular combination of cognitive skills and knowledge sampled by these tests plays a significant role in much of what goes on in modern industrialized societies. The concept of a segment of intellectual skills, albeit a broadly applicable and widely demanded segment, is replacing the notion of a general, univeral human intelligence.

A particularly relevant series of studies, begun in the 1970s and still in progress, is provided by the research on validity generalization conducted by Frank Schmidt, John Hunter, and their associates (Pearlman and others, 1980; Schmidt and others, 1979; Schmidt and others, 1981). Through sophisticated statistical analyses of data from many samples and from a large number of occupational specialties, these investigators are demonstrating that the validity of tests of verbal, numerical, and reasoning aptitudes can be generalized far more widely across occupations than had heretofore been recognized. The variations in validity coefficients typically found in earlier industrial studies can be ascribed largely to the effects of small sample sizes, restriction of range through preselection, and low reliability of criterion measures. The variance of obtained validity coefficients proved to be no greater than would be expected by chance from these three sources. This was true even when the particular job functions appeared to be quite dissimilar across jobs. Evidently, the successful performance of a wide variety of occupational tasks depends in large part on a common core of cognitive skills.

The tests surveyed in these studies covered chiefly the type of content and skills sampled in traditional intelligence and scholastic aptitude tests. It would seem that this cluster of cognitive skills and knowledge is widely predictive of performance in both academic and occupational activities. Their broadly generalizable predictive validity can probably be understood if we think of the tests operating at three levels. First, they permit a direct assessment of prerequisite intellectual skills demanded by many important tasks in our culture. Second, they assess the availability of a relevant store of knowledge or content also prerequisite for many educational and occupational tasks. Third, they provide an indirect index of the extent to which the individual has developed effective learning strategies, problem-solving techniques, and work habits and utilized them in the past. The effectiveness of this past behavior is reflected in the fullness of the individual's current store of knowledge and the readiness with which relevant knowledge can be retrieved. In at least three ways, therefore, performance on such tests provides clues about the resources available to an individual for subsequent learning, problem solving, and related activities.

Contributions from Related Fields

In addition to traditional psychometric studies, our understanding of what intelligence tests measure has been enriched in recent years by contributions from other areas of psychology and from related disciplines. Let me cite specifically cross-cultural psychology, developmental psychology, and cognitive psychology.

Cross-Cultural Psychology. Research in cross-cultural psychology demonstrates that there are, not one, but many kinds of intelligence (Berry, 1972; Goodnow, 1976; Neisser, 1976, 1979). For instance, cultures differ in the value they place on generalization and on the search for common features in disparate experiences. In some cultures, behavior is more specifically linked to contexts and situations than is true in the cultures within which most intelligence tests have been developed. Thus, the response may depend on who asks a question and on what type of content is involved. The individual may have learned to apply a particular operation, such as grouping or counting, to one type of content but not to another. Cultural differences in task interpretation may also influence what individuals select from their available response repertoire. For instance, functional classification in terms of use, such as placing a knife with an orange, may be chosen because it is considered more appropriate and sensible than classification into superordinate abstract classes, such as placing a knife with tools and an orange with fruit (Glick, 1975).

Viewing the diverse concepts of intelligence from a different angle, Neisser (1976, 1979) proposes that intelligence is not a quality of a person but a resemblance to a prototype. And he proceeds to show that there are multiple prototypes of the "intelligent person" across cultures. Even within our own culture, he differentiates between what he calls natural, "real-life" intelligence and academic intelligence. The former is quite diversified; it is closely adapted to specific situations; and it is influenced by the individual's own interests and goals. Academic intelligence, in contrast, is essentially what traditional intelligence tests measure. And it is important in school achievement and in many other activities that depend on formal schooling. Some fifty years ago Carl Brigham introduced the term "scholastic aptitude" to designate the test he developed for the College Board, the now well-known Scholastic Aptitude Test (SAT). He preferred this more narrowly descriptive term to the then current designation of intelligence test. The term "academic intelligence" serves the same delimiting function, suggesting that it is only one domain of intellectual functioning that is under consideration.

Some sociologists have coined the term "modern consciousness" to describe the psychological effects of being reared and educated in advanced industrial societies (P. L. Berger and others, 1973). This concept has been applied also to an examination of what intelligence tests measure. When thus viewed, intelligence tests can be said to assess the extent to which the individual has internalized "the cognitive requirements of the modern technological-rationalistic world" (B. Berger, 1978,

p. 35). An example of such cognitive requirements is a high level of abstraction, whereby each element of knowledge can be viewed apart from its immediate context.

A similar view has been expressed by Olson (1976), who observes that intelligence tests measure how well the individual has mastered the techniques of abstraction and rationality, which "are to a large extent the necessary but unintended consequences of technological developments" (pp. 200–201). Olson argues that the invention of a particular technology may alter the cognitive activities that constitute intelligence, and he illustrates this point with the invention of phonetic writing systems. He contrasts oral tradition with written language as a means of codifying and preserving the knowledge of a culture. Oral transmission concentrates on persons, events, aphorisms, and commandments; it is not well-adapted to the formulation of principles, laws, and formulas. With the introduction of written language, meaning became less dependent on context or on shared prior knowledge.

If we wish to understand and describe the intelligence of different cultures, we need naturalistic observations to identify the cognitive demands of particular environments. A task analysis of the behavioral requirements of a given culture (or subculture) represents an appropriate first step in constructing an intelligence test to assess how well individuals have acquired the skills and knowledge valued in that culture. If, however, we want an intelligence test to facilitate mobility into another environment, it is the cognitive demands of *that* environment that are relevant. The test should then be constructed from a task analysis of the new environment to which the individual wishes to move—whether it be an educational institution, an academic program, a vocational career, a country to which one is emigrating, or an emerging technology in a developing nation. One approach tells us how individuals arrived where they are in intellectual development; the other tells us what they need in order to go where they want to be.

Developmental Psychology. Within developmental psychology, the recent revival of interest in the work of Jean Piaget is well known. Apart from its specialized methodologies for assessing intelligence, the Piagetian approach has made significant contributions to our understanding of the nature of intelligence across the life span. Essentially, Piaget's observations suggest that intelligence may be qualitatively different at different life periods. This conclusion has found considerable support in the work of other investigators, especially those studying the behavior of infants and young children (Bayley, 1968, 1970; Lewis, 1973; Lewis and McGurk, 1972; McCall and others, 1972).

Such findings are also consistent with the concept of developmental tasks proposed by several psychologists in a variety of contexts

(Erikson, 1950; Havighurst, 1953; Super and others, 1957). Educationally and vocationally, as well as in other aspects of daily life, the individual encounters typical behavioral demands and problems at different life stages. For our present purpose, developmental psychology provides evidence, from several sources, that the definition of intelligence may vary across the life span. What intelligence tests measure—and what they ought to measure—may differ qualitatively at different life stages from infancy through adulthood.

Cognitive Psychology. As for cognitive psychology, it is helping to bridge the long-standing gap between psychometrics and experimental psychology. Beginning in the 1950s, cognitive psychologists have been applying the concepts of information processing to describe what occurs in human problem solving. Some have designed computer programs that carry out these processes and thereby simulate human thought. In the late 1960s and 1970s, a few psychologists began to apply these information-processing and computer-simulation techniques to an exploration of what intelligence tests measure (Carroll, 1976; E. Hunt, 1976; E. Hunt and others, 1976; Simon, 1976; Sternberg, 1979). Individual investigators have approached this goal from several different angles, and the research is still in an early exploratory stage. Thus far, information-processing approaches have contributed heuristic concepts to guide further research and have clearly focused attention on processes rather than end-products in problem solving. Analyzing intelligence test performance in terms of basic cognitive processes should certainly strengthen and enrich our understanding of what the tests measure. Moreover, analyzing individuals' performance at the level of elementary component processes may eventually make it possible to pinpoint each person's sources of weakness and strength and thereby enhance the diagnostic use of tests (Estes, 1974; Pellegrino and Glaser, 1979; Sternberg, 1979). This in turn should facilitate the tailoring of training programs to the individual's needs.

Training and Test Performance

Thus far I have been trying to clarify one aspect of my topic: why focus on intelligence tests, in what sense is the term intelligence being used, and why specify academic intelligence? Now we are ready to turn to the diverse effects of training. The main thrust of this paper is on the word "diverse." It is my contention that different kinds of training interventions have very different effects, consequences, and implications.

In evaluating the effects of training on test scores, a fundamental question is whether the improvement is limited to the particular items included in the test or whether it extends to the broader behavior domain that the test is designed to assess. The answer to this question represents the difference between coaching and education. Obviously, any educational experience the individual undergoes, either formal or informal, in or out of school, should be reflected in his or her performance on tests that sample relevant aspects of behavior. Such broad influences will in no way invalidate the test, since the test score presents an accurate picture of the individual's standing in the abilities under consideration. The difference, of course, is one of degree. Influences cannot be classified as either narrow or broad. They vary widely in scope, from those affecting only a single administration of a single test, through those affecting performance on all items of a certain type, to those influencing the individual's performance in the large majority of his or her activities.

From the standpoint of effective testing, however, a workable distinction can be made. Thus, we can say that a test score is invalidated only when a particular experience raises the score without appreciably affecting the behavior domain that the test samples. With this simple guideline as a starting point, we can examine the implications of three types of training intervention: coaching, test-taking orientation, and instruction in basic intellectual skills.

Coaching. The effects of coaching on test scores have been widely investigated. Several early studies were conducted by British psychologists, with special reference to the effects of practice and coaching on the tests formerly used in assigning eleven-year-old children to different types of secondary schools (Yates and others, 1953–1954). As might be expected, the extent of improvement depended on the ability and earlier educational experiences of the examinees, the nature of the tests, and the amount and type of coaching provided. Individuals with deficient educational backgrounds are more likely to benefit from special coaching than those who have had superior educational opportunities and are already prepared to do well on the tests. It is obvious, too, that the closer the resemblance between test content and coaching material, the greater will be the improvement in test scores. On the other hand, the more closely instruction is restricted to specific test content, the less likely it is that improvement will extend to criterion performance.

Although the term "coaching" was used by the investigators themselves, these early British studies span a wide range of procedures. In view of the age of the subjects and the time period covered (the early 1950s), much of the training may have been simply test-taking orientation. In the case of students with deficient educational backgrounds, some remedial education and training in basic skills may also have been included. Although I maintain that the three types of training can and should be differentiated in practice, I recognize that the term "coaching" is often used loosely to cover all three. We simply have to be alert to what was actually done in each instance, regardless of what it was called.

In the United States, the College Board has for many years been concerned about the spread of ill-advised commercial coaching courses for college applicants. Such courses fit more closely under coaching as I have used the term, in the sense of intensive concentrated drill or "cramming" on sample test questions. To clarify the issues, the College Board has conducted several well-controlled experiments to determine the effects of such coaching on its SAT, and has surveyed the results of similar studies by other investigators (Angoff, 1971; College Entrance Examination Board, 1979a, 1979b). These studies covered a variety of coaching methods and included students in both public and private high schools. Large samples of minority students from both urban and rural areas were also investigated. The general conclusion from such studies was that intensive drill on items similar to those on the SAT is unlikely to produce appreciably greater gains than those that occur when students are retested with the SAT after a year of regular high school instruction.

It should also be noted that in its regular test construction procedures, the College Board investigates the susceptibility of new item types to coaching (Angoff, 1971; Pike and Evans, 1972). Item types on which performance can be appreciably raised by short-term drill or by instruction of a narrowly limited nature are not retained in the operational forms of the tests. Examples of item types excluded for this reason are artificial language and number series completion. Another obvious example is provided by problems that call for an insightful solution which, once attained, can be applied directly to solving similar problems. When encountered in the future, such problems would test recall rather than problem-solving skills. A familiar illustration is the water-jug problem. Once individuals have caught on to the idea of emptying one jug into another one or more times, they can solve all these problems.

From another angle, it should be added that, on the basis of its training studies, the College Board recommends that students who are not enrolled in a mathematics course at the time they take the SAT can benefit from a review of the math concepts they learned in class. This would come under the heading of education rather than coaching. In the verbal domain, such review did not have an appreciable effect, probably because verbal reasoning is such an integral part of the students' daily lives that it has less chance of becoming rusty from disuse.

Test-Taking Orientation. Next we can consider the effects of test sophistication or sheer test-taking practice. In studies with alternate forms of the same test, there is a tendency for the second score to be higher. Significant mean gains have been reported when alternate forms were administered in immediate succession or after intervals ranging from one day to three years (Angoff, 1971; Droege, 1966; Peel, 1951, 1952). Similar results have been obtained with normal and intellectually gifted schoolchildren, high school and college students, and employee samples. Data on the distribution of gains to be expected on a retest with a parallel form should be provided in test manuals, and allowance for such gains should be made when interpreting test scores.

Nor are score gains limited to alternate forms. The individual who has had extensive prior experience in taking standardized tests enjoys a certain advantage in test performance over one who is taking his or her first test (Millman and others, 1965; Rodger, 1936). Part of this advantage stems from having overcome an initial feeling of strangeness as well as from having developed more self-confidence and better test-taking attitudes. Part is the result of a certain amount of overlap in the type of content and functions covered by many tests. Specific familiarity with common item types and practice in the use of objective answer sheets may also improve performance slightly. It is particularly important to take test sophistication into account when comparing the scores obtained by persons whose test-taking experience may have varied widely.

Short orientation and practice sessions can be quite effective in equalizing test sophistication (Wahlstrom and Boersman, 1968). Such familiarization training reduces the effects of prior differences in test-taking experience as such. Since these individual differences are specific to the test situation, their diminution should permit a more valid assessment of the broad behavior domain the test is designed to measure. This approach is illustrated by the College Board publication entitled *Taking the SAT* (College Entrance Examination Board, 1981), a booklet distributed since 1978 to all college applicants who register for this test. The booklet offers suggestions for effective test-taking behavior, illustrates and explains the different types of items included in the test, and reproduces a complete form of the test, which students are advised to take under standard timing conditions and to score with the given key.

More general test-orientation procedures have also been developed. An example is the *Test Orientation Procedure,* designed chiefly for job applicants with little prior testing experience (Bennett and Doppelt, 1967). It comprises a booklet and tape recording on how to take tests, with easy test-like exercises; and a second, twenty-page booklet of sample tests which the prospective applicant can take home for practice. The United States Employment Service also has prepared a booklet on how to take tests, as well as a more extensive pretesting orientation technique for use with educationally disadvantaged applicants who are tested at state employment services (U.S. Department of Labor, 1968, 1970, 1971).

Instruction in Broad Intellectual Skills. Some researchers have been exploring the opposite approach to the improvement of test performance. Their goal is the development of widely applicable intellectual skills, work habits, and problem-solving strategies. The effect of such interventions should be manifested in *both* test scores and criterion performance, such as college courses. This type of program is designed to provide education rather than coaching. And it is concerned with the modifiability of intelligence itself.

Contrary to the still prevalent popular notion regarding the fixity of the IQ, there is a growing body of evidence that the behavior domain sampled by intelligence tests is responsive to training. It is interesting to note that, despite subsequent misinterpretations of the Binet scales, Binet himself rejected the view that intelligence is unchangeable. He and his associates developed procedures, which they called "mental orthopedics," for raising the intellectual level of mental retardates. As early as 1911, Binet wrote that for "children who did not know how to listen, to pay attention, to keep quiet, we pictured our first duty as being . . . to teach them how to learn" (Binet, 1911, p. 150).

The decades of the 1960s and 1970s witnessed a strong upsurge of interest in programs for improving academic intelligence. These programs were developed largely in the United States and in Israel, where there were large minority populations that were having difficulty in adapting to the majority culture. By far the largest number of these programs was directed at the infant and preschool levels (B. Brown, 1978; Consortium for Longitudinal Studies, 1978; Day and Parker, 1977; J. McV. Hunt, 1975; Peleg and Adler, 1977). These educational programs ranged widely in content and quality. A few were well designed and are relevant to the present topic insofar as they endeavored to develop cognitive skills judged to be prerequisite for subsequent schooling. It is these programs that yielded the most promising results. The more successful also included parental involvement as a means of supplementing the preschool experiences and ensuring their continuation after the program terminates.

Other programs, on a smaller scale, have been designed for school-age children (Bloom, 1976; Jacobs and Vandeventer, 1971; Olton and Crutchfield, 1969; Resnick and Glaser, 1976). Although these programs are still at a research stage, their preliminary findings are encouraging. Some investigators have focused on still older age levels, working with college and professional school students (Bloom and

Broder, 1950; Whimbey, 1975, 1977). It is noteworthy that they, too, report significant improvement in academic achievement and in performance on scholastic aptitude tests. Still other investigators have concentrated on educable mentally retarded children and adolescents, with results that have both theoretical and practical implications (Babad and Budoff, 1974; Belmont and Butterfield, 1977; A. L. Brown, 1974; Budoff and Corman, 1974; Campione and Brown, 1979; Feuerstein, 1979). Some investigators have even been conducting exploratory research on such training effects with profoundly retarded children, and they too report promising results (Tryon and Jacobs, 1980).

At all age levels, these programs have been directed primarily to persons from educationally disadvantaged backgrounds. In connection with his work with mental retardates in Israel, Feuerstein (1979) offers a provocative definition of cultural deprivation. He identifies the culturally deprived as persons who have become alienated from their own culture through a disruption of intergenerational transmission and mediational processes. As a result, they have failed to acquire certain learning skills and habits that are required for high-level cognitive functioning. Culturally different persons, on the other hand, having learned to adapt to their own culture, have developed the prerequisite skills and habits for continued modifiability and can adapt to the demands of the new culture after a relatively brief transition period. The same concept underlies Whimbey's work with college students. Designating his approach as "cognitive therapy," Whimbey observed that it resembles "the type of parent-child verbal dialogue in problem solving that researchers believe constitutes the academic advantage middle-class children have over lower-class children" (Whimbey, 1975, p. 68).

Another important concept that emerges from this training research is that of self-monitoring. This is reminiscent of Binet's inclusion of self-criticism as a component of intelligent behavior (Binet, 1911, p. 122). Whimbey (1975, pp. 137–138) also emphasizes the need for training in this process in view of the high frequency of shoddy, careless, and impulsive responses among poor test performers. Flavell (1979) has devoted special attention to cognitive monitoring under the broader heading of metacognition, or the individual's knowledge about himself or herself and other persons as cognitive processors.

The training research on intelligence has yielded some provocative concepts and some promising procedures for developing the academic intelligence measured by traditional tests. Improvement can occur at considerably later ages than heretofore anticipated. But the later the training is begun, the more limited will be its effectiveness. Through special training programs, one can learn widely applicable cognitive skills, problem-solving strategies, efficient study habits, and other useful behavioral processes. It takes a long time, however, to accumulate the relevant content store in long-term memory, which is also a part of intelligence and which contributes to the person's readiness to learn more advanced material. Although the older person, armed with efficient learning techniques, can build up this content store more quickly than he or she would have as a child, it is nevertheless unrealistic to expect this to occur after short training periods distributed over a few months. There are no shortcuts to intellectual development—at least not *that* short! It is well to bear this limitation in mind. Otherwise, if unrealistic expectations remain unfulfilled, there is danger that disillusionment will weaken confidence in the entire training approach. Intelligence *can* be improved at any age, but the earlier one begins, the greater will be the returns from one's efforts.

Implications for Test Validity. We have considered three approaches to the improvement of test performance, whose objectives are clearly differentiable. How do these types of training affect the validity of a test and its practical usefulness as an assessment instrument? The first was coaching, in the sense of intensive, massed drill on items similar to those on the test. Insofar as such coaching might improve test performance, it would do so without a corresponding improvement in criterion behavior. Hence it would thereby reduce the test's predictive validity. Test-orientation procedures, on the other hand, are designed to rule out or minimize differences in prior test-taking experience. These differences represent conditions that affect test scores as such, without necessarily being reflected in the broader behavior domain to be assessed. Hence the test-orientation procedures should make the test a more valid instrument by reducing the influence of test-specific factors. Finally, training in broadly applicable intellectual skills, if effective, should improve the trainee's ability to cope with subsequent intellectual tasks. This improvement will and should be reflected in test performance. Insofar as both test scores and criterion performance are improved, such training leaves test validity unchanged.

References

Angoff, W. H. (Ed.). *The College Board Admissions Testing Program: A Technical Report on Research and Development Activities Relating to the Scholastic Aptitude Test and Achievement Tests.* New York: College Entrance Examination Board, 1971.

Babad, E. Y., and Budoff, M. "Sensitivity and Validity of Learning-Potential Measurement in Three Levels of Ability." *Journal of Educational Psychology,* 1974, *66,* 439–447.

Bayley, N. "Behavioral Correlates of Mental Growth: Birth to Thirty-Six Years." *American Psychologist*, 1968, *23*, 1–17.

Bayley, N. "Development of Mental Abilities." In P. Mussen (Ed.), *Carmichael's Manual of Child Psychology*. Vol. 1. New York: Wiley, 1970.

Belmont, J. M., and Butterfield, E. C. "The Instructional Approach to Developmental Cognitive Research." In R. V. Kail, Jr. and J. Hagen (Eds.), *Perspectives on the Development of Memory and Cognition*. Hillsdale, N.J.: Erlbaum, 1977.

Bennett, G. K., and Doppelt, J. E. *Test Orientation Procedure*. New York: Psychological Corporation, 1967.

Berger, B. "A New Interpretation of the IQ Controversy." *The Public Interest*, 1978, No. 50, 29–44.

Berger, P. L., Berger, B., and Kellner, H. *The Homeless Mind: Modernization and Consciousness*. New York: Random House, 1973.

Berry, J. W. "Radical Cultural Relativism and the Concept of Intelligence." In L. J. Cronbach and P. J. D. Drenth (Eds.), *Mental Tests and Cultural Adaptations*. The Hague: Mouton, 1972.

Binet, A. *Les Idées Modernes sur les Enfants*. Paris: Flammarion, 1911.

Bloom, B. S. *Human Characteristics and School Learning*. New York: McGraw-Hill, 1976.

Bloom, B. S., and Broder, L. *Problem-Solving Processes of College Students*. Chicago: University of Chicago Press, 1950.

Brown, A. L. "The Role of Strategic Behavior in Retardate Memory." In N. R. Ellis (Ed.), *International Review of Research in Mental Retardation*. Vol. 7. New York: Academic Press, 1974.

Brown, B. (Ed.). *Found: Long-Term Gains from Early Intervention*. Boulder, Colo.: Westview Press, 1978.

Budoff, M., and Corman, L. "Demographic and Psychometric Factors Related to Improved Performance on the Kohs Learning Potential Procedure." *American Journal of Mental Deficiency*, 1974, *78*, 578–585.

Campione, J. C., and Brown, A. L. "Toward a Theory of Intelligence: Contributions from Research with Retarded Children." In R. J. Sternberg and D. K. Detterman (Eds.), *Human Intelligence: Perspectives on Its Theory and Measurement*. Norwood, N.J.: Ablex, 1979.

Carroll, J. B. "Psychometric Tests as Cognitive Tasks: A New 'Structure of Intellect.'" In L. B. Resnick (Ed.), *The Nature of Intelligence*. Hillsdale, N.J.: Erlbaum, 1976.

College Entrance Examination Board. *Taking the SAT: A Guide to the Scholastic Aptitude Test and the Test of Standard Written English*. New York: College Entrance Examination Board, 1981. (1st ed., 1978).

College Entrance Examination Board. *The Admissions Testing Program Guide for High Schools and Colleges, 1979–81*. New York: College Entrance Examination Board, 1979a.

College Entrance Examination Board. "The Effect of Special Preparation Programs on Score Results of the Scholastic Aptitude Test." *Research and Development Update*, January 1979b. (Also reprinted in *The College Board News*, February 1979, p. 7.)

Consortium for Longitudinal Studies. *Lasting Effects after Preschool*. Washington, D.C.: U.S. Government Printing Office, 1978.

Day, M. C., and Parker, R. K. (Eds.). *The Preschool in Action: Exploring Early Childhood Programs*. Boston: Allyn & Bacon, 1977.

Droege, R. C. "Effects of Practice on Aptitude Scores." *Journal of Applied Psychology*, 1966, *50*, 306–310.

Erikson, E. H. *Childhood and Society*. New York: Norton, 1950.

Estes, W. K. "Learning Theory and Intelligence." *American Psychologist*, 1974, *29*, 740–749.

Feuerstein, R. *The Dynamic Assessment of Retarded Performers*. Baltimore, Md.: University Park Press, 1979.

Flavell, J. H. "Metacognition and Cognitive Monitoring: A New Area of Cognitive-Developmental Inquiry." *American Psychologist*, 1979, *34*, 906–911.

Glick, J. "Cognitive Development in Cross-Cultural Perspective." In F. D. Horowitz (Ed.), *Review of Child Development Research*. Vol. 4. Chicago: University of Chicago Press, 1975.

Goodnow, J. J. "The Nature of Intelligent Behavior: Questions Raised by Cross-Cultural Studies." In L. B. Resnick (Ed.), *The Nature of Intelligence*. Hillsdale, N.J.: Erlbaum, 1976.

Havighurst, R. J. *Human Development and Education*. New York: Longmans, Green, 1953.

Hunt, E. "Varieties of Cognitive Power." In L. B. Resnick (Ed.), *The Nature of Intelligence*. Hillsdale, N.J.: Erlbaum, 1976.

Hunt, E., Frost, N., and Lunneborg, C. "Individual Differences in Cognition." In G. Bower (Ed.), *The Psychology of Learning and Motivation: Advances in Research and Theory*. Vol. 7. New York: Academic Press, 1973.

Hunt, J. McV. "Reflections on a Decade of Early Education." *Journal of Abnormal Child Psychology*, 1975, *3*, 275–330.

Jacobs, P. I., and Vandeventer, M. "The Learning and Transfer of Double-Classification Skills: A Replication and Extension." *Journal of Experimental Child Psychology*, 1971, *12*, 140–157.

Lewis, M. "Infant Intelligence Tests: Their Use and Misuse." *Human Development*, 1973, *16*, 108–118.

Lewis, M., and McGurk, H. "Evaluation of Infant Intelligence: Infant Intelligence Scores—True or False?" *Science*, 1972, *178* (4066), 1174–1177.

McCall, R. G., Hogarty, P. S., and Hurlburt, N. "Transitions in Infant Sensorimotor Development and the Prediction of Childhood IQ." *American Psychologist*, 1972, *27*, 728–748.

Millman, J., Bishop, C. H., and Ebel, R. "An Analysis of Test-Wiseness." *Educational and Psychological Measurement*, 1965, *25*, 707–726.

Neisser, U. "General, Academic, and Artificial Intelligence." In L. B. Resnick (Ed.), *The Nature of Intelligence*. Hillsdale, N.J.: Erlbaum, 1976.

Neisser, U. "The Concept of Intelligence." *Intelligence*, 1979, *3*, 217–227.

Olson, D. R. "Culture, Technology, and Intellect." In L. B. Resnick (Ed.), *The Nature of Intelligence*. Hillsdale, N.J.: Erlbaum, 1976.

Olton, R. M., and Crutchfield, R. S. "Developing the Skills of Productive Thinking." In P. H. Mussen, J. Langer, and M. Covington (Eds.), *Trends and Issues in Developmental Psychology*. New York: Holt, Rinehart & Winston, 1969.

Pearlman, K., Schmidt, F. L., and Hunter, J. E. "Test of a New Model of Validity Generalization: Results for Job Proficiency and Training Criteria in Clerical Occupations." *Journal of Applied Psychology*, 1980, *65*, 373–406.

Peel, E. A. "A Note on Practice Effects in Intelligence Tests." *British Journal of Educational Psychology*, 1951, *21*, 122–125.

Peel, E. A. "Practice Effects Between Three Consecutive Tests of Intelligence." *British Journal of Educational Psychology*, 1952, *22*, 196–199.

Peleg, R., and Adler, C. "Compensatory Education in Israel: Conceptions, Attitudes, and Trends." *American Psychologist,* 1977, *32,* 945–958.

Pellegrino, J. W., and Glaser, R. "Cognitive Correlates and Components in the Analysis of Individual Differences." *Intelligence,* 1979, *3,* 187–214.

Pike, L. W., and Evans, F. R. "Effects of Special Instruction for Three Kinds of Mathematics Aptitude Items." *College Entrance Examination Board Research Report* 1, 1972.

Resnick, L. B. (Ed.). *The Nature of Intelligence.* Hillsdale, N. J.: Erlbaum, 1976.

Resnick, L. B., and Glaser, R. "Problem Solving and Intelligence." In L. B. Resnick (Ed.), *The Nature of Intelligence.* Hillsdale, N.J.: Erlbaum, 1976.

Rodger, A. G. "The Application of Six Group Intelligence Tests to the Same Children, and the Effects of Practice." *British Journal of Educational Psychology,* 1936, *6,* 291–305.

Schmidt, F. L., Hunter, J. E., Pearlman, K., and Shane, G. S. "Further Tests of the Schmidt-Hunter Bayesian Validity Generalization Procedure." *Personnel Psychology,* 1979, *32,* 257–281.

Schmidt, F. L., Hunter, J. E., and Pearlman, K. "Task Differences as Moderators of Aptitude Test Validity in Selection: A Red Herring." *Journal of Applied Psychology,* 1981, *66,* 161–185.

Simon, H. A. "Identifying Basic Abilities Underlying Intelligent Performance of Complex Tasks." In L. B. Resnick (Ed.), *The Nature of Intelligence,* Hillsdale, N.J.: Erlbaum, 1976.

Sternberg, R. J. "The Nature of Mental Abilities." *American Psychologist,* 1979, *34,* 214–230.

Super, D. E., and others. *Vocational Development: A Framework for Research.* New York: Teachers College Press, 1957.

Tryon, W. W., and Jacobs, R. S. *"Effects of Basic Learning Skill Training on Peabody Picture Vocabulary Test Scores of Severely Disruptive, Low-Functioning Children."* Paper presented at the meeting of the Eastern Psychological Association, Hartford, Conn., April 1980.

U.S. Department of Labor, Employment and Training Administration. *Pretesting Orientation Exercises (Manual; Test Booklet).* Washington, D.C.: U.S. Government Printing Office, 1968.

U.S. Department of Labor, Employment and Training Administration. *Pretesting Orientation on the Purposes of Testing (Manual; Illustrations).* Washington, D.C.: U.S. Government Printing Office, 1970.

U.S. Department of Labor, Employment and Training Administration. *Doing Your Best on Aptitude Tests.* Washington, D.C.: U.S. Government Printing Office, 1971.

Wahlstrom, M., and Boersman, F. J. "The Influence of Test-Wiseness upon Achievement." *Educational and Psychological Measurement,* 1968, *28,* 413–420.

Whimbey, A. *Intelligence Can Be Taught.* New York: Dutton, 1975.

Whimbey, A. "Teaching Sequential Thought: The Cognitive-Skills Approach." *Phi Delta Kappan,* 1977, *59,* 255–259.

Yates, A. J., and others. "Symposium on the Effects of Coaching and Practice in Intelligence Tests." *British Journal of Educational Psychology,* 1953, *23,* 147–162; 1954, *24,* 57–63.

Anne Anastasi is Professor Emeritus of psychology in the Graduate School of Arts and Sciences, Fordham University. A past president of the American Psychological Association, she is the author of Differential Psychology *(3rd ed., 1958),* Fields of Applied Psychology *(2nd ed., 1979), and* Psychological Testing *(5th ed., 1982). In 1981, she received the APA Distinguished Scientific Award for the Applications of Psychology.*

*Does coaching improve scores on the SAT? This is not a
yes-no question; it is a matter of degree.*

The Controversy over Coaching: Issues of Effectiveness and Equity

Samuel Messick

The controversy over whether or not coaching works for tests of scholastic aptitude such as the College Board SAT is in actuality a multitude of
controversies—over the meaning of scholastic aptitude, the meaning of
coaching, the nature of the fundamental research questions, the adequacy of the empirical evidence for coaching effectiveness, the possible
implications of effective coaching for student performance and for test
validity, and the consequent ethical imperatives for educational and testing practice. Since misconceptions and misunderstandings abound on

A longer version of this chapter appears in the ETS Research Report Series
as RR 81–19, Princeton, N.J.: Educational Testing Service. I wish to thank Albert
Beaton, Thomas Donlon, Garlie Forehand, Norman Frederiksen, and Robert
Linn for their helpful comments on the manuscript and George Miller, Donald
Rock, Ledyard Tucker, and Howard Wainer for their advice on various aspects of
analysis. Special thanks go to Ann Jungeblut for her pervasive contributions to the
substance and phrasing of this work.

B. F. Green (Ed.), *New Directions for Testing and Measurement: Issues in
Testing—Coaching, Disclosure, and Ethnic Bias*, no. 11. San Francisco:
Jossey-Bass, September 1981.

every one of these points, discussions of the coachability of scholastic aptitude tests readily reduce to rhetorical and political posturing when what is needed is more extensive rational analysis and scientific appraisal of research evidence. And as we shall see, since much of the controversy reflects poorly articulated ethical stances, what is also needed is a clearer conception of the values underlying rival ethical imperatives.

In any event, it is not so much a question of eschewing rhetoric, because in essence test "validation is a rhetorical process" (Cronbach, 1980, p. 102). Rather, it is a question of ensuring that the rhetorical arguments reflect facts and rationales as well as values and beliefs. Granted that "empirical evidence, task analysis, formal assumptions, everyday beliefs, and valuations are intertwined in the argument that supports a test use" (Cronbach, 1980, p. 101; Messick, 1980b, 1981b), nonetheless the role of evidence should be central and directive in tempering the trade-offs embodied in our current best scientific judgment about a value-laden issue such as coaching. To be sure, since it rarely completely dispels divergent interpretations, evidence—that is, "both data, or facts, and the rationale or arguments that cement those facts into a justification of . . . inferences" (Messick, 1980b, p. 1014)—may not fully determine the outcome or conclusion. Evidence does serve, however, to limit the range of *plausible* alternatives. In an attempt to reinforce the directive role of evidence in current arguments over coaching, the present chapter summarizes research findings from studies of coaching for the SAT in the context of a conceptual analysis of the meaning and likely import of the coachability of such ability tests. The intention is to illuminate if not resolve, in the light of recent research results, the central issues of meaning, effectiveness, and equity of access inherent in the coaching controversy.

Controversies Over Meaning

As so often happens in continuing controversies, the key terms— in this case "coaching" and "scholastic aptitude"—take on different meanings for different proponents. Multiple meanings of test constructs often lead to surplus or excess meanings that go beyond defensible score interpretations, and "excess meanings lead to misuses and misinterpretations of tests" (Anastasi, 1980, p. 1). Imputed meanings for coaching range all the way from short-term cramming and simple practice on sample items at one extreme to long-term instruction aimed at knowledge and skill development at the other. Similarly, imputed meanings for scholastic aptitude range all the way from "fixed endowment," which implies that valid scholastic aptitude tests should be essentially uncoachable, to "direct learning outcome," which implies that they should be as responsive to coaching or instruction as any other measure of educational achievement such as tests of history or biology. But scholastic aptitude as measured by the SAT falls at neither of these two extremes. The SAT measures developed—or more precisely, developing—abilities that are by no means fixed but which, by the senior year of high school, are relatively stable in their development. This implies that the SAT may indeed be responsive to coaching or instruction to some degree, but it should not be nearly as responsive as the typical educational achievement test of subject-matter attainment.

   Scholastic Aptitude as Developed Ability. One important source of controversy over the meaning of scholastic aptitude derives from differences in the popular and technical uses of the term "aptitude." The dictionary (Webster, 1969) denotes aptitude as "capacity for learning . . . [or] natural ability" (p. 44), and "a natural liking for some activity and the likelihood of success in it" (p. 352). In the loose language of popular usage, it seems only a small slip to move from "natural ability" to "innate ability" and from there to "fixed ability." But it is a slip nonetheless and, from the standpoint of its putative implications for aptitude measurement, an enormous one. Because if aptitude constitutes fixed ability, then valid aptitude tests presumably should not be coachable. Any such tests that in fact prove to be coachable are not valid measures of aptitude by this chain of reasoning, but rather assess general educational achievement; they should therefore be treated in selection decisions on the same basis as other measures of achievement. If purported aptitude tests are interpreted as being more fundamental or more instrumental in predicting future success than are typical achievement tests, and if those so-called aptitude tests are indeed coachable, then the issue comes to be cast in terms of fair test use. By this line of argument, coachable aptitude tests are ipso facto unfair to students not having access to high quality coaching programs. But the equity issue is much more complicated than this (even granting the foregoing simplistic premises) because coaching is a form of instruction, and coachable aptitude tests are said to be akin to achievement tests which are expected to be responsive to instruction—in this involuted sense of unfairness where tests bear the burden for societal inequities, educational achievement tests have always been unfair to students not having access to high quality *instructional* programs.

   In contrast to nontechnical dictionaries, a compendium of psychological terms (English & English, 1958) asserts that "aptitude (which formerly carried implications of *innateness*) has now been specialized in technical writing to refer to the fact that the individual can be brought by a specified amount of training to a specified level of *ability,* either general or special" (p. 1). Furthermore, "an aptitude test is merely one form of ability test, . . . a measure of present characteristics that has been found to be predictive of capacity to learn" (p. 39) or, more generally, predictive of future performance. Along these same lines, two closely related but distinct features of aptitude are noted by Cronbach and Snow (1977): Generally speaking, aptitude is "any characteristic of a person that forecasts his probability of success under a given treatment" (p. 6), that is, aptitude is a *forecaster* of learning or performance; speaking "psychologically, aptitude is whatever makes a person ready to learn rapidly in a particular situation" (p. 107), that is, aptitude is a *facilitator* of learning or performance. Both of these connotations are inherent in the typical rationales for interpretation and use of scholastic aptitude tests.

Scholastic aptitude tests such as the SAT are not direct measures of innate intelligence or fixed endowment, nor are they measures of subject-matter attainment as in the usual educational achievement test. The SAT was designed explicitly to differ from achievement tests in subject-matter fields in the sense that its content, being derived from a wide variety of substantive areas, is not tied to a particular field of study, curriculum, or program. The SAT measures developed abilities of verbal and mathematical reasoning and comprehension that are acquired gradually over many years of experience and use in both school and nonschool settings, being exercised to some degree in all subject-matter areas at all levels of schooling as well as in response to real-life situations. According to Carroll (1978), "to the extent that tests of the SAT type are valid in predicting college or graduate-school success, it is undoubtedly because they provide a good indication of the extent to which applicants have *at the time of testing* developed or acquired, and can exhibit through their performance on a test, certain general intellectual skills in handling verbal, quantitative, and symbolic information that are contributory or even necessary to high-level success in academic studies" (p. 78). In other words, scholastic aptitude tests are general forecasters of academic learning and performance because they measure general facilitators of academic learning and performance.

A critical feature of this technical formulation of the construct of aptitude is that scholastic aptitudes are viewed as developed abilities, not fixed abilities, so one might expect high quality instruction over an extended period of time to improve them. But since these general intellective skills develop gradually over a number of years as a result of every-day experience as well as formal education, they may be relatively difficult to enhance markedly in late adolescence through brief courses of intervention. This is in contradistinction to the specific knowledge and skills tapped by typical educational achievement tests, which should be relatively responsive to high quality instruction even in the short run.

As Carroll (1978) put it, "a low score on . . . a [scholastic aptitude] test is no guarantee that the individual cannot acquire, during a subsequent period, the skills and abilities that are tested, but it is an indication, at least, of the probability that the individual could acquire these skills and abilities, if at all, only with much expense of time and effort and with careful instruction" (p. 78).

Repeatedly throughout this discussion, contrasts have been drawn between scholastic ability tests on the one hand and educational achievement tests on the other. In idealized form, these two types of tests define opposite poles of a continuum, with most actual educational tests (by virtue of sharing various features of each pole) falling somewhere in the intermediate range. For example, scholastic ability tests measure general intellective skills such as verbal reasoning by means of diverse content drawn from a multiplicity of topical areas, whereas educational achievement tests measure specialized knowledge and skill using relatively circumscribed content drawn from a particular subject-matter field. Yet an achievement test in political science, say, might include items to assess skill in reasoning with political concepts; to the extent that such specific reasoning also reflects more general reasoning abilities, the test might prove to be more broadly predictive beyond political science to related fields.

Coaching as Instruction, Demonstration, and Practice. Just as there is a progression or ordering of educational tests ranging from measures of scholastic abilities at one pole to measures of subject-matter attainment at the other, so there is a progression of types of preparation for taking examinations ranging from practice on sample tests at one extreme to intensive instruction aimed at developing knowledge and skill at the other. Historically, coaching for scholastic ability tests has tended to fall toward the practice side of this continuum, emphasizing test familiarization and test-taking strategies, while coaching for achievement tests has tended to fall toward the instructional side, emphasizing directed study and review of subject-matter content. This wide array of possible forms of coaching has led to heated controversy over its meaning because different parties often selectively restrict their referents to different portions of the continuum. At the same time, the full range of coaching possibilities has come to be applied to any type of educational test, thereby making preferential usage appear not only restrictive but arbitrary. For example, in regard to coaching for the SAT, some writers have limited their use of the term to short-term drill, test practice, and test-wiseness training (compare Pike, 1978), whereas others include under the same rubric virtually full-time instruction at specialized preparatory schools for periods of six months or more (compare Slack and Porter, 1980). Adherents of the former position underscore a distinction between coaching and instruction, whereas adherents of the latter position view such differences as immaterial, implying that anything resulting in improved test scores testifies to coachability.

In an effort to avoid disputes over what is or is not coaching, here we will accept as coaching any intervention procedure specifically undertaken to improve test scores, whether by improving the skills measured by the test, by improving the skills for taking the test, or both. Thus, for our purposes coaching may fall anywhere in the broad range bounded by the two extremes of practice and instruction, embracing any combination of test familiarization, drill-and-practice with feedback, motivational enhancement, training in strategies for specific item formats and for general test taking (including advice on pacing, guessing, and managing test anxiety), subject-matter tuition and review, and skill-development exercises. In this view, coaching for educational tests is any procedure specifically oriented toward the improvement of test scores as distinct from nontest-specific learning experiences and cognitive growth— which may also result in improved test scores. This broadly inclusive stance is consistent with the dictionary definition of the word coaching, which is "to train intensively by instruction, demonstration, and practice" (Webster, 1969, p. 158).

Controversies Over Effectiveness

Even if we were to have agreement on the meaning of scholastic aptitude as developed ability and on the meaning of coaching as any intervention procedure for improving test scores, there would still be ample controversy over the effectiveness of coaching and, indeed, over the way in which the question of effectiveness is posed. As Kaplan (1964) maintains, "How we put the question reflects our values on the one hand, and on the other hand helps determine the answer we get" (p. 385). The challenge is to have sufficient recourse to relevant research evidence so that our values do not *solely* determine the answer we get. The problem is that research evidence is selectively sought in the context of the question posed so that facts and values are intimately intertwined in our efforts at interpretation. One safeguard is to attempt to take values explicitly into account throughout the research endeavor. Another is to pose the research question in alternative ways so that data are collected and analyzed from alternative perspectives in the hope that convergence of evidence will lead to consensus of interpretation and that divergence of evidence will lead to exposure and examination of value differences (Churchman, 1971, 1979; Messick, 1975, 1980b).

Yes-No Questions Versus Questions of Degree. Studies of the effectiveness of coaching for the SAT have consistently posed the research question in categorical form, seeking to ascertain in general terms whether or not coaching works and, if it does, to determine the overall amount of score increment attainable through coaching (Messick, 1980a). Those viewing the coachability of scholastic aptitude tests as primarily an issue of fair testing practice tend to phrase the question in this way. For them, coachability implies unfairness if student access to effective coaching is not equitable or, at the least, if examinees are not uniformly apprised of the kinds of special preparation they should undertake. However, if coachability is viewed not only as an issue of fair testing practice but also as an issue in the construct validity of scholastic aptitude tests as measures of developing abilities, then the research question is more aptly posed as one of degree: It is not just a question of whether or not coaching works, but of how much student time and effort devoted to what kinds of coaching experiences yield what level of score improvements. From this standpoint, it matters to what *degree* coaching is effective and by what *means,* for although developed scholastic abilities may be further developed by relatively long-term programs emphasizing comprehension and reasoning skills, they should not be readily improved by short-term programs stressing test-taking strategies or drill-and-practice. This is not to say, however, that programs of the latter type might not lead to some score improvement as a consequence of enhanced test wiseness or reduced anxiety about what to expect.

The first viewpoint, by virtue of focusing simplistically on whether or not coaching works, leads to a simple tallying of statistically significant and nonsignificant coaching effects, or to an averaging of attained coaching effects across available studies (Slack and Porter, 1980). The second viewpoint, by virtue of focusing on the relationship between student time and effort devoted to coaching and the size of associated score effects, leads to the calculation of correlation coefficients across coaching programs between estimated coaching effects and such indices of student effort as program contact time (Messick & Jungeblut, 1981). Each of these viewpoints thus provides a distinctive organizing framework for summarizing the research findings from studies of coaching for the SAT, which is our next topic for detailed examination. One might hope that such a juxtaposition of alternative ways of integrating research findings would provide some closure on the issue of coaching effectiveness—and it does—but the situation is beclouded by a variety of flaws in experimental design that variously distort the extant studies. This leads to yet another controversy, this time over the adequacy of the empirical evidence for coaching effectiveness.

Categorical Answers Versus Relational Answers. Whether posed in categorical or in relational terms, the question of coaching effectiveness must be answered in comparative terms by appraising obtained score gains associated with coaching against the baseline of experiential growth in ability that may occur over the same time period in the absence of any coaching program. Since developed scholastic abilities continue to develop during the high school years in response to both formal schooling and nonschool experiences, any score increases exhibited by groups of coached students need to be evaluated in comparison with the score gains of equivalent control groups of uncoached students. A major source of discord in summarizing the import of research results on coaching is that several of the studies either utilized no control group at all or employed control groups that were seriously nonequivalent to the treatment groups, thereby rendering highly questionable both the size and the meaning of obtained score effects.

In the former case, in the absence of control groups, there is no really satisfactory way to adjust the obtained score increases for expected experiential growth in ability, although various adjustments based on comparisons with national norm groups or with control groups from similar studies have been attempted with debatable credibility. In the latter case of nonequivalent control groups, regression techniques may be used to control statistically for those group differences for which some index or measure is available, but there is no way of adjusting for any unmeasured personal characteristics that might have influenced both the student's participation in the coaching program and that program's apparent effectiveness.

This is the problem of selection bias, which is a pervasive one in studies of coaching. It arises whenever systematic differences that are correlated with the dependent variable, in this case with SAT performance, exist between the experimental and control samples. Systematic differences resulting from student choice of the treatment rather than from experimenter choice of the student are called self-selection bias. To be sure, those group differences for which reliable measures are available may be effectively adjusted statistically using analysis-of-covariance techniques, but to the extent that unmeasured group differences are also likely, residual selection bias remains and the results are invariably equivocal. For example, in the Federal Trade Commission (FTC) study (1979), the coached group differed dramatically from the uncoached group on a number of indices related to SAT performance such as having higher school grades and parental income, making it likely that they also differed on equally pertinent unmeasured factors such as motivation and parental education. Under these circumstances, the obtained score effects cannot be unequivocally attributed to the coaching treatment and must be interpreted as combined coaching/self-selection effects (Messick, 1980a; Stroud, 1980).

The standard prescription for avoiding selection bias is an experimental design with random assignment of participants to coached treatment groups and noncoached control groups, for only with random assignment can treatment effects be presumed to be independent of prior status on any of a host of personal or background characteristics. At the outset, no systematic differences are expected between treatment and control groups when they are constituted by random assignment, and if effective control conditions are instituted and maintained, the only systematic difference that should eventuate is that the treatment group will have been coached while the control group will not.

To date, three studies of SAT coaching have employed random assignment (Alderman and Powers, 1980; Evans and Pike, 1973; Roberts and Oppenheim, 1966) and, given the power of randomized experiments to obviate selection bias, one might ordinarily expect heavy reliance to be placed on their results. However, in all three instances the posttest used was a special administration of a retired form of the SAT or PSAT (Preliminary Scholastic Aptitude Test) rather than a regular SAT administration. In each case, for purposes of equity, the plan was to make coaching available to all study participants but to postpone access for the control groups until after the experimental posttest; the intent of administering a special SAT was to protect the control students from having test scores count on their college admission records before they had an opportunity to be coached. But, precisely because they did not count, these special administrations may have been viewed to some degree as practice tests, thereby eliciting less motivation and effort than a real SAT administration, especially for the uncoached control students.

Warning signals that this might have been the case were detected in two of the studies (Alderman and Powers, 1980; Roberts and Oppenheim, 1966), in which some of the control groups were found to exhibit score *decreases* in going from the pretest to the special SAT posttest when the expectation from national norm samples of test repeaters is for score *increases* over the same time period. Decreases in control-group scores were not observed in the third randomized study (Evans and Pike, 1973) or, for that matter, in all of the schools included in the other two investigations. Control-group scores in 3 out of 14 schools did not decrease in the Roberts and Oppenheim study; while 5 out of 8 did not decrease in the Alderman and Powers study. But there is no way of gauging how much the obtained score increases were influenced by the different motivational conditions of a special, as opposed to a regular, SAT.

Although the available studies of SAT coaching are methodologically flawed in one way or another, the various defects entail sufficiently divergent implications that any regularities or lawful consistencies across the studies would nonetheless be compelling. Most of the studies are subject to the influence of selection bias discussed earlier, which severely compromises interpretations as to the source or determinants of score effects—in particular whether they may be unequivocally attributed to coaching experiences as opposed to personal or background characteristics of the (self-)selected students. In this regard, some of the studies involved control groups of uncoached students attending different schools from those of the coached students or else drawn from other extrinsic sources such as test-score files, thereby confounding coaching effects with school effects and numerous self-selection factors (Dear, 1958; Dyer, 1953; Federal Trade Commission, 1979; French, 1955; Stroud, 1980). In some other studies, control groups of uncoached students were specially constituted to match available samples of commercially coached students on a number of variables, but this still allows systematic differences between the groups on unmatched variables (Frankel, 1960; Whitla, 1962).

Another defect common to several of the studies is an unfortunate reliance on small samples of coached students, which results in imprecise estimates of score effects and a reduced likelihood that real effects will be detected as statistically significant (Alderman and Powers, 1980; Coffman and Parry, 1967; Frankel, 1960; Whitla, 1962). Moreover, as we have seen, some studies were subject to the unrealistic motivational conditions of a special as opposed to a regular SAT administration, which very likely introduced biases in the estimated sizes of score effects (Alderman and Powers, 1980; Evans and Pike, 1973; Roberts and Oppenheim, 1966). Finally, and by far the most troublesome from the standpoint of estimating and interpreting coaching effects, some of the studies had no control groups at all (Coffman and Parry, 1967; Marron, 1965; Pallone, 1961).

All of these studies are arrayed in Table 1, which lists for each coaching program the type of control-group design employed, the size and statistical significance of the obtained score effect, the amount of student contact time entailed, and the size of experimental and control samples. This information is given separately for the Verbal (V) and Math (M) parts of the SAT. The studies are grouped into three sections in order to obtain separate estimates of average score effects from those studies having control groups, those without control groups, and those manifesting some evidence of distorted or biased results. Included in this latter group are those coaching programs that exhibited control-group score decreases (Alderman and Powers,1980; Roberts and Oppenheim, 1966) as well as the study by Coffman and Parry (1967), which was marred by treatment-group score decreases and other indications of motivational difficulties. The estimates of score effect and of student contact time in Table 1 are as given in Messick and Jungeblut (1981), in which each of the studies is summarized in detail. The score effects for the control-group studies are either weighted intercept differences between experimental and control regression lines, when these were available from analyses of covariance, or else they are weighted average score increases of experimental over control groups, weighted in the case of multiple experimental or control groups by their respective sample sizes. The score effects for the uncontrolled studies were estimated by reducing the reported score gains by an amount approximating the corresponding experiential growth expected on the basis of both national norms data and control-group growth in similar studies. For details see Messick and Jungeblut (1981).

To begin with, we note that a simple tallying of statistically significant and nonsignificant score effects is not very illuminating. Of the 17 Verbal score effects derived from control-group studies (including the suspect ones), 5 are statistically significant at the .05 or .01 level and 12 are not, but 10 of the latter values are based on treatment-group sizes of about 50 cases or less compared with more than 100 cases for each of the significant effects. Of the 12 Math score effects from control-group studies, 8 are statistically significant (all but one at the .01 level) and 4 are not significant, two of the latter being based on coached samples of 50 or fewer cases. Although such tallies of significant and nonsignificant findings may tell us more about the size of samples and about the power of statistical tests than about the effectiveness of coaching, even this gross comparison tends to suggest that SAT-Verbal (SAT-V) may be somewhat less responsive to coaching interventions than SAT-Math (SAT-M), which should not surprise us given the greater curriculum relatedness of SAT-M.

Inquiring about the average sizes of obtained score effects is not very helpful either, because one gets strikingly different answers from those studies having some form of control group versus those studies having no control group at all. Excluding the suspect studies and weighting in each case by the size of the associated coached sample, the weighted average SAT-V effect from control-group studies is 14.4 and that of SAT-M is 16.2, whereas the corresponding values from the uncontrolled studies are 39.0—or 36.6 (see Table 1)—and 54.2. These values represent average numbers of SAT score points on a score scale ranging from 200 to 800 points on which typical score distributions exhibit standard deviations of about 100 points.

Since the uncontrolled studies yield estimated score effects that are far out of line with those of the control-group studies, we must carefully appraise the credibility of the adjustments made for experien-

Table 1. SAT Score Effects in Relation to Student Contact Time in Coaching Studies With and Without Control Groups

Verbal

Study	Control Group Design	Score Effect	Student Contact Time in Hours	N Exp/Control
Dyer (1953)	Different School	4.6*	10	225/193
French (1955) V & M	Different School	18.3**	8.3	161/158
French (1955) Vocabulary	Different School	5.0*	4.5	110/158
Dear (1958)	Same and Different Schools	-2.5^{ns}	6	60/526
Frankel (1960)	Same School Statistically Matched	8.4^{ns}	15	45/45
Whitla (1962)	Statistically Matched	11.0^{ns}	5	52/52
FTC (1979; Stroud, 1980) School A	Test-Score Files	31.7**	20	393/1729
School B	Test-Score Files	5.2^{ns}	12	163/1729
Alderman & Powers (1980)				
School C	Randomized	-2.75^{ns}	10.5	22/17
School E	Randomized	-.64^{ns}	6	25/74
School F	Randomized	.63^{ns}	5	37/35
School G	Randomized	18.01^{ns}	11	24/70
School H	Randomized	12.16^{ns}	45	16/19

14.4 weighted average (13 studies)

Math

Study	Control Group Design	Score Effect	Student Contact Time in Hours	N Exp/Control
Dyer (1953)	Different School	12.9**	8.3	225/193
French (1955)	Different School	11.0**	8.3	161/268
Dear (1958) Long	Same and Different Schools	23.6**	12	71/116
Dear (1958) Short	Same and Different Schools	21.5**	6	60/526
Frankel (1960)	Same School Statistically Matched	9.4^{ns}	15	45/45
Whitla (1962)	Statistically Matched	-5.3^{ns}	5	50/50
FTC (1979; Stroud, 1980) School A	Test-Score Files	24.9**	20	393/1729
School B	Test-Score Files	7.5^{ns}	12	163/1729
Evans & Pike (1973)				
Group QC	Randomized	11.0*	21	145/129
Group DS	Randomized	19.0**	21	72/129
Group RM	Randomized	25.0**	21	71/129

16.2 weighted average (11 studies)

Pallone (1961)				
Short	None	81	45	20+
Long	None	68(43)[a]	100[b]	80–
Marron (1965)				
Group 1	None	54	300	83
Group 2	None	33	300	600
Group 3	None	24	300	5
Group 4	None	12	300	26
		39.0(36.6)[a] weighted average (6 studies)		

RANK-ORDER CORRELATION   .77 (19 studies)

Roberts & Oppenheim (1966)	Randomized	14.4*	3.8	154/111
Alderman & Powers (1980)				
School A	Randomized	28.39^{ns}	7	28/22
School B	Randomized	7.94^{ns}	10	39/40
School D	Randomized	6.82^{ns}	10	48/43
Coffman & Parry (1967)	None	4	48	19
		12.9 Weighted average (5 studies)		

RANK-ORDER CORRELATION   .62 (24 studies)

Marron (1965)				
Group 1'	None	59	300	232
Group 2'	None	53	300	405
Group 3'	None	46	300	78
		54.2 weighted average (3 studies)		

RANK-ORDER CORRELATION   .71 (14 studies)

Roberts & Oppenheim (1966)	Randomized	8.1^{ns}	3.8	188/122

RANK-ORDER CORRELATION   .74 (15 studies)

[a] Because of a 25-point discrepancy between the values reported in Pallone's (1961) text and tables, it is not clear which score effect is correct; both are reported here along with the corresponding weighted averages.

[b] Since students in this coaching course were also attending preparatory school full time, the amount of Verbal contact time might be more appropriately estimated as 300 hours (Messick & Jungeblut, 1981).

* Significance level $<.05$ ** Significance level $<.01$ ns Nonsignificant

tial growth in lieu of control-group comparisons, for at first glance these uncontrolled studies appear to warrant a more general discounting on methodological grounds alone. We must also consider the possibility that even though the score effects from the uncontrolled studies are out of line with those from the controlled studies, they may be in line with expectations derived from systematic program differences between the two types of studies; in particular, the fact that the coaching programs in the control-group studies, with one exception, entailed about 20 hours of student contact time or less, whereas the programs in the uncontrolled studies, again with one exception, entailed about 300 hours of student contact time.

However, before addressing these two questions in detail—that is, how defensible are the estimated score effects from the uncontrolled studies and how credible are they as student outcomes from long-term coaching programs?—we should first consider a further complication. In some cases, the program score effects reported in Table 1 obscure emergent interactions between the size of individual score effects and the personal or background characteristics of the students (Dear, 1958; Dyer, 1953; French, 1955; Stroud, 1980). This sporadic emergence of statistically significant interactions indicates that certain types of students, such as those with low family income or males not currently studying math, might exhibit larger than average score increases in some coaching programs (Messick, 1980a). These are particular instances of a more general possibility that we should now be ever alert to—that coaching programs, like other forms of teaching, may display differential effects for different types or groups of students.

Since particular types of students may exhibit larger than average score effects in some coaching programs and since the score effects exhibited in the uncontrolled studies were larger than the average effects obtained in the control-group studies, the discrepancy in the average size of effects in the two kinds of studies may be partly attributable to student differences as well as to program differences and design differences. This brings us to the two questions that were temporarily left in abeyance—how defensible are the corrections for experiential growth used in estimating score effects in the uncontrolled studies and how plausible are those adjusted score effects as student gains in ability due to coaching? The interpretive difficulties introduced by the complete absence of control groups were indeed compounded by the special and self-selected nature of the students in the uncontrolled studies. These studies (Marron, 1965; Pallone, 1961) were each conducted in private preparatory schools that specialized in providing high school graduates with a year of post-high school study aimed at securing admission to the

U.S. service academies and selective colleges (the school involved in Pallone's investigation was one of the ten studied by Marron).

In the absence of control groups of similar students, it is difficult to appraise the import of the obtained score gains. Four methods of adjusting for experiential growth in ability over the pretest-posttest interval have been suggested as a means of salvaging these studies, but these proposals are all questionable for one reason or another. The authors of the original articles both suggested that the obtained score increases be compared with normal expectations of SAT gains typical of males during the senior year of secondary school as revealed by College Board normative data (Marron, 1965; Pallone, 1961). This is not a very satisfactory comparison, however, because the preparatory school students in question, most of whom were high school graduates, were clearly not representative of high school seniors who take the SAT. Another suggestion was to compare the obtained results with average gains in national SAT administrations of junior- to senior-year retesters having the same initial average score levels as the preparatory school students (Slack and Porter, 1980). Again, this is not a very satisfactory comparison because these private school students were not a representative sample of the national population of test repeaters. Other suggestions involved a comparison of the original score increases with the average gains of control students in superior schools from other studies of proprietary programs (Pike, 1978) or with score gains of control students in other coaching studies who had average initial score levels roughly comparable to Pallone's and Marron's groups (Messick and Jungeblut, 1981).

The point is that in the absence of comparable control groups no generally satisfactory estimate of coaching or instructional effects can be made. But the fact is that these four proposed adjustments, though based on different and debatable rationales, yield corrections for experiential growth that are not radically different from one another. The lowest estimates of experiential growth were generally produced by the Slack and Porter (1980) procedure and the highest by Pike's (1978); on the average, the former fell about 10 points below the mean of all four adjustments and the latter fell about 8 points above the mean. The correction applied to each uncontrolled study in Table 1 was the average of all four proposed procedures (Messick and Jungeblut, 1981). This resulted in weighted average estimates of experiential growth in Pallone's case of 41 SAT-V points over a twelve-month testing interval and, in Marron's case, of 23 SAT-V points and 25 SAT-M points over a six-month testing interval. Given the highly self-selected nature of the preparatory school students and the fact that these gross procedures leave important factors of differential motivation and growth uncontrolled, these provisional values for experiential growth may still be somewhat underestimated—and the corresponding adjusted score effects some- what overestimated—but they do not seem to be unreasonable. Indeed, they appear to be in the right ballpark.

The resulting weighted average score effects from the uncon- trolled studies were 39 points for SAT-Verbal and 54 points for SAT- Math, which brings us to the question of how credible it is to find such large score effects associated with SAT coaching programs. Of course, with such highly self-selected students—and especially in the absence of control groups or refined covariance adjustments—these score effects represent combined coaching/self-selection effects, and their size may be as much a consequence of student characteristics as of program effec- tiveness. On the other hand, the preparatory school programs in ques- tion were not typical SAT coaching efforts, but rather entailed "full-time exposure to course content that is directly related to the verbal and mathematics College Board tests (both aptitude and achievement)" (Marron, 1965, p. 1), undertaken "for students in their final year of precollege work, including a large number of high school graduates who were completing a year of post-high school study" (Pallone, 1961, p. 655). It should come as no surprise if such a long-term instructional program with curriculum emphases on test-relevant knowledge and skill de- velopment were found to yield larger SAT score gains than short-term programs emphasizing test familiarization and practice, as is the situation with some of the control-group studies in Table 1. If this is the case, then the search for categorical answers to the simplistic question of whether or not coaching works is seen to be futile, for the computation of an overall average score effect across the range of studies in Table 1 would produce a misleading middle ground that fails to characterize the results of either the long-term or the short-term programs very well.

As a consequence, there is little recourse but to seek relational answers to more complex questions of degree. Instead of appraising the average size of score effects associated with coaching in general, we should rather appraise the size of particular score effects in relation to the amount and kind of coaching by asking how much student time and effort devoted to what kinds of coaching experiences yield what level of score improvements. In this approach, a natural first step is to correlate the size of obtained score effects with available indices of program characteristics. Unfortunately, data on program characteristics that are sufficiently commensurable across studies to permit a detailed compari- son and evaluation of coaching procedures is typically not available. Indeed, no coaching study as yet has systematically investigated the *kinds* of instructional methods and materials that may be most effective in improving SAT performance. Although program descriptors that apply uniformly across studies are rare in the literature on coaching for the SAT, the amount of student contact time in each coaching program does provide a generally applicable index of student effort. Since, for the relevant research studies, those coaching programs involving relatively high amounts of student contact time also entailed structured curricula emphasizing knowledge and skill development while the relatively low-contact programs emphasized test review and practice, this index embodies a confounding of program characteristics in these data. Thus, student contact time in this context can also be viewed as a proxy for increasing curriculum structure and increasing emphasis on skill development.

When all of the studies in Table 1 are ranked in order of their obtained score effects and this ranking is compared with their ordering in terms of student contact time in the respective coaching programs, the two rank orders prove to be remarkably similar. As seen in Table 1, the Spearman rank-order correlation coefficient between SAT-V score effect and student contact time across all 24 Verbal coaching studies is .62, while that for SAT-M across all 15 Math coaching studies is .74. Both coefficients are statistically significant at the .01 level. If the five suspect studies are deleted from the calculation for SAT-V, the new correlation is .77 across 19 studies, which is also significant at the .01 level. Thus, as anticipated, the suspect studies add considerable noise to the data set, but the relationship between SAT-V score effect and student contact time remains strong with or without them. The results for SAT-M, in contrast, are hardly affected by the lone suspect Math coaching study; upon its deletion, the new correlation is .71 across 14 Math studies, which again is significant at the .01 level.

In interpreting these sizable correlation coefficients, it must be remembered that as rank-order statistics they imply a regular monotonic relationship between student contact time and score effect but not necessarily a linear one. Indeed, even though the time dimension is covered in only a fragmentary fashion by the available studies, when the magnitude of score effect is plotted against student contact time, the relationship is distinctly nonlinear. To demonstrate this, when linear regression lines were fit to score effects from coaching programs requiring less than 50 hours of student contact time (all of which included control groups), the extrapolated predicted score effects for coaching programs entailing 300 hours of contact time (none of which included control groups) were much higher than the score effects actually obtained. In the case of SAT-V, the predicted 300-hour score effects consistent with linearity were two to three times as large as the obtained average score effects, whether actual or adjusted, and for SAT-M, three to four times as large.

This marked linear overprediction of score effects for higher values of student contact time clearly indicates a phenomenon of diminishing returns in coaching effectiveness (Messick and Jungeblut, 1981).

Diminishing Returns in SAT Coaching Effects. As is frequently the case with diminishing returns, a logarithmic transformation of the time dimension provided a much better representation of the functional relationships. To illustrate, when linear equations were fit to the regression of score effect on *log* contact time for those coaching programs requiring less than 50 hours, the extrapolated predicted values for 300-hour programs (33 points for Verbal and 44 points for Math) now deviated from the corresponding obtained average adjusted score effects by only about 3 to 5 points for SAT-V, depending on which of Pallone's (1961) discrepant values are included, and by 10 points for SAT-M. Regression lines fit to all of the data in log time were very similar to those regression lines based only on control-group studies, differing from each other by only 2 or 3 points for SAT-V and 8 points for SAT-M at the benchmark of 300 hours (Messick and Jungeblut, 1981). These logarithmic equations based on the full range of data (excluding the suspect studies and Pallone's discrepant values) are plotted in Figure 1, transformed so as to relate SAT score effect to student contact time in real rather than log hours.

As can be seen from Figure 1, according to the logarithmic models fit to the obtained score effects from the available SAT coaching studies, a Verbal coaching program involving about 10 hours of student contact time would be expected to be associated with average SAT-V score effects of 8 or 9 points, while a 10-hour Math coaching program would be associated with average SAT-M effects of about 12 or 13 points. Similarly, the corresponding values for a 20-hour Verbal and a 20-hour Math program are 13 SAT-V points and 21 SAT-M points; for 30-hour programs apiece, 16 SAT-V points and 25 SAT-M points; for 50 hours each, 19 and 31 points; for 100 hours each, 24 and 39 points; for 200 hours each, 28 and 47 points; and, for 300 hours each, 31 and 52 points. Or for uniform 10-point increases in expected average score effect, the associated hours of contact time would be as follows: About 12 hours of Verbal coaching or 8 hours of Math coaching for an average of 10 SAT points; about 57 hours of Verbal or 19 hours of Math coaching for an average of 20 score points; about 260 hours of Verbal or 45 hours of Math for an average of 30 points; and, about 1,185 hours of Verbal or 107 hours of Math for an average of 40 points. Thus, arithmetically increasing amounts of score effect are associated with geometrically increasing amounts of student contact time. For uniform 10-point increases in average score effect, as in the illustration just presented, the multiplicative constant carrying one amount of student contact time into the next higher amount is about 4.57 for SAT-V and about 2.37 for SAT-M. The

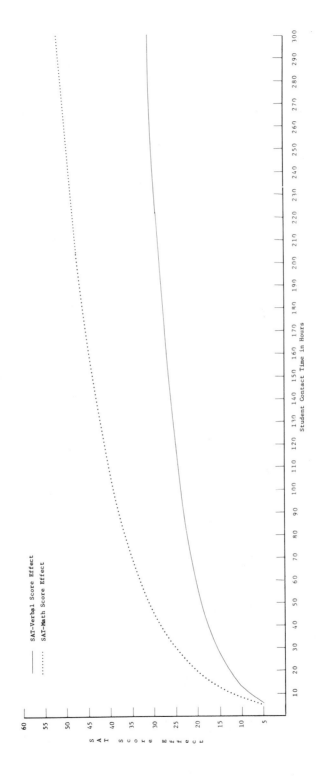

Figure 1. Expected SAT Score Effects Associated with Given Hours of Student Contact Time Separately for Verbal and Math According to the Logarithmic Models Fit to Available Coaching Data (i.e., 20 hours of Verbal Coaching Yields an Expected Score Effect of About 13 SAT-V Points; and, Another 20 Hours of Math Coaching Yields an Expected SAT-M Score Effect of About 21 Points)

fact that Verbal entails much more student contact time than Math for the same amount of average score effect—at least for these logarithmic models fit to available SAT coaching data—is consistent once again with the expectation that Math, being more curriculum related than Verbal, should be relatively more responsive to coaching intervention.

It must be emphasized that these logarithmic functions are based on existing data from available studies, all of which involved students who to a large degree were motivated to increase their test scores through coaching. Since such motivated students are likely to have been highly task oriented, it is not unreasonable under these circumstances that student contact time should be found to be directly related to average test score increases (Stallings, 1980). But we must remember two cautionary notes: one, that increases in student contact time are confounded in these studies with increasing curriculum emphases on knowledge and skill development, so that other program characteristics that contact time may be a proxy for should also be taken into account in interpreting the relationships and determining expectations. The other derives from the pervasiveness of methodological flaws in the extant studies, which compels us to consider the possible role of selection bias in interpreting the basis of the functional relationships. Many of the longer-term programs, such as the preparatory schools in Marron's (1965) study and commercial coaching school A in the FTC (1979) study, were not only associated with larger score effects but were also highly subject to self-selection bias. With these caveats in mind, it appears likely that improvement of the comprehension and reasoning skills measured by the SAT, when it occurs, is a function of the time and effort expended and that each additional score increase may require geometrically increasing amounts of time and effort. This developmental pattern of gradual and diminishing increases in response to coaching or instructional experiences is just about what one might expect with measures of stable, though *developing* abilities.

Controversies Over Implications

Before we can properly appraise the import of an apparently curvilinear relationship between student contact time and score effects associated with coaching, we must carefully consider the different ways in which coaching might operate to improve test scores. With respect to implications for educational and testing practice, it matters what processes underlie improved test performance—in particular, whether any increased test scores attributable to coaching reflect stable improvements in the verbal and mathematical reasoning abilities measured by the SAT as opposed to improved facility in overcoming inadvertent sources of test difficulty unrelated to these reasoning skills (such as test anxiety or unfamiliarity with different item formats and test-taking strategies), or some combination of the two. We must also consider the extent to which any obtained score increases associated with coaching are practically worthwhile in relation to the investment of student time, effort, and cost required and in light of multitudinous factors that complicate this judgment. Depending on their source and practical utility, SAT score gains attributable to coaching—if they were to occur with any regularity— would have important policy implications for either educational practice or testing practice, or both.

Implications for Student Performance and Test Validity. Of the potential ways in which coaching may function to improve test scores, three major possibilities can be distinguished (Messick, 1980a): First, some coaching programs may genuinely improve the abilities and skills measured by the test, resulting in commensurate increases in test scores. Such score increases reflective of improved abilities should threaten neither the construct validity nor the predictive utility of the SAT, for any lasting improvements in verbal and quantitative reasoning abilities should lead to score increases on tests measuring these constructs and should also serve the student well in criterion situations entailing these abilities, as is the case in school and college learning. Second, some coaching programs may enhance test-taking sophistication or reduce the anxiety often associated with taking tests, resulting in increased test scores that are now more accurate assessments of student ability. Such score increases reflective of improved test wiseness, by virtue of revising previous scores that were inaccurately low because of construct-irrelevant test difficulty, should lead not only to more accurate assessment of abilities but also to enhanced predictive validity of the test. Third, some coaching programs may teach test-taking stratagems and answer-selection tricks, resulting in increased test scores that are inaccurately high as assessments of student ability. Such score increases reflective of acquired artifice should not only dilute the construct validity of the test but jeopardize its predictive validity as well. Some coaching programs, of course, may produce none of these effects or more than one in various combinations, so that in any particular instance some mix of improved abilities, improved test wiseness, and improved artifice might contribute to improved test performance.

The first two possible outcomes, if they were realized, would be good both from the standpoint of student performance and from the standpoint of test validity. The third possibility is probably only a minor problem with well-constructed tests, because professional test makers strive to minimize the use of complicated or tricky item formats and to avoid items that may be answered on the basis of clues unrelated to the abilities tested. Moreover, test makers also strive to attenuate the import of the second possible outcome of coaching by providing test-familiarization materials and practice tests to all candidates as well as advice on guessing, pacing, reviewing, and the like.

Thus, of three main possible outcomes of coaching, two are good for both student performance and test validity while the third is a minor and rarely demonstrable problem with professionally developed tests. The second possibility—that improved test wiseness might yield increased test scores of greater accuracy—although potentially critical for certain types of students who are relatively unpracticed and unoriented in the ways of standardized testing, is of debatable importance for the generality of students. The principal reason for this surmise is that various coaching programs have attempted to enhance test wiseness by drilling the student in different approaches to different item formats and to allay anxiety by providing feedback on effective item performance, but the available fragmentary research evidence indicates that if this is all that is done such coaching will have little impact on SAT scores (Messick, 1980a). Coaching programs that emphasize test familiarization and practice appear to be associated with small score effects, if any, whereas programs that include skill-development components tend to be associated with larger score effects which, on the whole, seem to occur more for Math than for Verbal. This can be seen in Table 1 once we note that the former programs tend to be relatively short-term while the latter programs are relatively long-term.

This leaves us with the first possible outcome of coaching—namely, that effective coaching programs genuinely improve the verbal and mathematical reasoning abilities measured by the SAT—and with the task of ascertaining the credibility of such an outcome given the paucity of directly relevant research evidence. No study of coaching to date has systematically addressed this issue of improved abilities. Rather, all of them have focused on the prior issue of first demonstrating significant score increases associated with coaching before inquiring into their causes. Since this second step has not yet been taken, we can only conjecture as to the likelihood that obtained score increases reflect improved reasoning skills.

An important related question pertains not only to the improvement of abilities through coaching but to the stability of that improvement over the long term. If effective coaching does improve abilities, this might occur via the development of new skills or, more likely, by the strengthening, honing, and refining of existing skills through exercise and challenge. Although increased test scores attributable to coaching may reflect real ability improvement at the time of testing, this improvement may be relatively enduring or transitory depending on whether critical levels of exercise and challenge are maintained in the student's learning environment until the ability gains become stably consolidated.

Since coached scores, if they indeed represent improvements in ability, should be just as valid or more valid than uncoached scores in predicting academic success, at least in the first year of college, one might turn to such predictive data if it existed for evidence of improved abilities. However, such an approach is both indirect and ineffectual. It is indirect because it requires not only that reasoning abilities be improved by coaching but that the improved skills be both durably maintained over the freshman year and effectively utilized in college performance, whereas numerous countervailing factors—such as social adjustment problems and heavy involvement in athletics or other extracurricular activities—may contribute to scholastic underachievement and the gradual erosion of academic skills. It is ineffectual with respect to inferences about improved abilities because the validity of coached scores might derive not from improved abilities but from improved accuracy in the assessment of existing abilities attained through enhanced test wiseness. Thus, high predictiveness would provide positive evidence that increased test scores attributable to coaching reflect either stable improvements in abilities or more accurately assessed abilities which in either case were well utilized in college performance, but low predictiveness would constitute negative evidence only if plausible alternative explanations for poor academic performance could be discounted.

Despite these interpretive pitfalls, one coaching study—that undertaken by Marron (1965) at ten specialized preparatory schools—tentatively explored this indirect route by appraising the extent to which SAT scores after long-term coaching predicted freshman class standings at the U.S. service academies and selective colleges. As a further complication, however, relatively crude and approximate methods of equating were required in Marron's study to achieve some semblance of distributional comparability across the service academies and across the widely diverse colleges that the preparatory students dispersed to. Although the outcome is thereby rendered admittedly tenuous, the findings nonetheless suggest that at the service academies the students did less well academically than the test scores predicted, whereas at the selective colleges the distributions of class standings and test scores did "not seem to be inconsistent" (Marron, 1965, p. 22).

Thus, the possibility that effective coaching may genuinely improve the comprehension and reasoning skills measured by the SAT is neither strongly supported nor strongly countered by available data, mostly because so little of it is directly pertinent to the issue. To assess even tentatively which way the existing data point, we must rely on indirect signals and bits of circumstantial evidence, most of which are discernible in Figure 1. After all, what research evidence there is about coaching for the SAT has been summarized in Table 1 and statistically integrated into the curves of Figure 1. Those curves suggest that SAT score effects—as embodied in a logarithmic model fitting the available fragmentary data—are still increasing, minutely but steadily, up to 300 hours of student contact time and beyond. Each additional amount of score increase entails geometrically more student contact time. This is a pattern more suggestive of developing abilities than of either enhanced test wiseness or acquisition of subject-matter knowledge.

Subject-matter achievement ought to increase at a faster or less diminishing rate in response to tuition, as indeed it did in Marron's (1965) study, in which weighted average score gains on achievement tests of English composition were almost one and a half times as large as unadjusted weighted average gains on SAT-V while gains on intermediate and advanced Math tests were roughly one and three-quarter times as large as on SAT-M. In contrast, it is most unlikely that enhanced test wiseness or anxiety reduction would still be accruing positive effects, however diminishing, after 300 hours or even 100 hours. Given the circumscribed nature of the information and advice to be imparted and the inevitable redundancy of repeated test practice per se, coupled with the modest results of coaching programs emphasizing test familiarization and item review, one might expect the effects of test-wiseness training alone to peak and level off within 10 to 20 hours of student contact time or less. After all, 10 to 20 hours of test-wiseness training would be comparable to a one-credit college course in test taking. Consistent with this conjecture, the faster initial growth rates in the curves of Figure 1 indeed suggest that score effects associated with the first 10 to 20 hours or so of student contact time may possibly reflect a combination of enhanced test wiseness and developing abilities, with the former becoming progressively less important and the latter progressively more important in the attainment of larger and larger score effects.

Implications for Guidance and Admissions. SAT score increases attributable to coaching, if they occur with any certitude, may have important implications not only for testing practice but also for educational practice—for learning and instruction as well as for guidance and admissions. Before we can ponder potential implications, however, we must confront the question of practical utility—how large does an obtained coaching effect need to be to have practical significance for various purposes? As we shall see, since a number of factors must be taken into account simultaneously, this is a complicated question which can only be answered conditionally. Nonetheless, it would help to clarify if not resolve the issue if we could underscore some of the relevant factors while at the same time discounting other ostensible answers that turn out to be largely irrelevant to the utility of coaching effects.

In this regard, one commonly mentioned benchmark is the standard error of measurement of the test, which typically hovers around 30 score points or so for both SAT-V and SAT-M. The standard error of measurement is the standard deviation of measurement errors from whatever source—of major concern in connection with a multiple-form test such as the SAT are those errors incumbent upon taking one test form as opposed to other parallel or equivalent forms. A range of plus or minus one or two standard errors of measurement around a student's observed score is usually taken as a confidence interval serving to bound, with a given probability, the student's true score. Compared with this band of plus or minus 30 to 60 points of expected error, most of the score effects associated with coaching programs in Table 1 appear to be relatively small. But these score effects, by and large, represent differences in average score increases of coached groups over control groups, which automatically takes the standard error of measurement into account since it operates in similar fashion in both the coached and uncoached samples.

From this perspective, the standard error of measurement is irrelevant to the appraisal of *average score effects* associated with coaching, because these effects reflect differences over and above the influence of measurement error. It is also largely irrelevant to the appraisal of *individual score effects* attributable to coaching, provided they are calculated as residual scores around regression lines based on uncoached or pooled samples, as in analysis of covariance (Cochran, 1968). Such residual scores also estimate coaching effects over and above the standard error of measurement, in addition to being adjusted for contaminating variance on any covariates included in the regression equation—although the size of the standard error does affect the size of the individual residuals. However, the standard error of measurement is by no means irrelevant to *individual score gains* calculated as simple differences between two testings before and after coaching. In this case, negative errors of measurement in the first testing coupled with positive errors in the second would inflate any coaching effect, whereas positive measurement errors in the first testing coupled with negative errors in the second would attenuate it.

Another reason why the standard error of measurement is not an apposite yardstick for gauging average coaching effects is that measurement error is a random process affecting all test takers irrespectively, whereas coaching is a deliberate and directed process selectively affecting only those test takers who engage in it. There is no question of unfairness in connection with error of measurement, for it constitutes the luck of the draw in how well the sample of items on a particular SAT form happens to match the individual's functional capabilities on a given day. That on a different day or a different test form the individual's score might be somewhat higher or somewhat lower is what is meant by error of measurement, and it applies to everyone on a randomly probabilistic basis. In contrast, demonstrably effective coaching, being systematic and selective rather than random and universal, would inevitably raise questions of unfairness; as we shall see when such questions are addressed in detail in the next section, however, they are neither new nor unique to coaching. Nonetheless, in terms of social implications, since a relatively large standard error universally applied might be tolerable while a same-sized coaching effect selectively applied might not, there are ethical as well as logical and statistical reasons to avoid comparing the two.

Other often invoked contexts for evaluating the size of coaching effects are the SAT score scale, which ranges from 200 to 800 points, and the number of additional items correct implicit in a given score effect. For example, a coaching effect of 20 SAT-V points corresponds to about three additional Verbal items correct while 20 SAT-M points corresponds to roughly two additional Math items correct. A 20-point coaching effect thus seems trivial when viewed in terms of additional items correct or in terms of a 600-point potential score range. But the choice of a score scale is arbitrary and, within the limits of adequate reliability and feasible testing time, so is the number of items in the test.

Although the 200- to 800-point SAT score scale is immaterial for gauging the size of coaching effects, the distribution of test scores along that scale is definitely not. In particular, the standard deviation of the SAT score distribution, which is normally in the neighborhood of 100 points for both SAT-V and SAT-M, provides a highly pertinent yardstick for assessing coaching impact. Although the numerical value of the standard deviation is tied to the arbitrary score scale (as is the metric of the coaching effects), what is not arbitrary is the number of standard deviation units that a given coaching effect represents. Thus, a 20-point coaching effect is roughly a fifth of a standard deviation of the score distribution, and it remains a fifth of a standard deviation under any linear transformation of the score scale.

By casting coaching effects in standard deviation units, we are in a position to translate score gains attributable to coaching into corresponding increases in percentile rank. That is, for normally distributed test scores in general, we can now determine the improvement in a student's percentile rank attendant upon a given score effect; but this percentile change is variable because it is contingent upon initial score level prior to coaching. For example, if the initial uncoached score were two standard deviations below the mean, a 20-point score effect would yield a percentile improvement of 1.3; if one standard deviation below the mean, a 20-point effect yields an improvement of 5.3 percentiles; at the mean, 7.9 percentiles; one standard deviation above the mean, 4.4 percentiles; and, two standard deviations above the mean, only .9 percentiles. Thus, the largest improvement in percentile rank occurs for initial scores at the mean of the score distribution, with the amount of improvement falling off as initial scores deviate from the mean in either direction. Furthermore, a given score effect yields slightly larger percentile improvements for initial uncoached scores below the mean in comparison with the improvements associated with corresponding scores equally far above the mean. Although the SAT score scale is not precisely normal and the standard deviation varies slightly from year to year, the corresponding percentiles and percentile changes in the 1979–1980 national percentile tables for college-bound seniors are within a point or two of these normal-curve values.

With respect to the practical consequences of such percentile improvements, we should note that low-scoring students, who most need whatever benefits coaching might accrue, gain relatively little in percentile rank from a 20-point score effect. The same holds true for high-scoring students, who nonetheless might strongly desire any additional benefits derivable from coaching if they aspire to highly selective colleges. Assuming a 20-point coaching effect, a student with an initial uncoached score 1.5 standard deviations below the mean would rise three percentiles (from a percentile rank of 7 to a rank of 10), whereas a student initially scoring 1.5 standard deviations above the mean would gain about two percentiles (from a percentile rank of 93 to 95). For scores initially at the 50th percentile, a 20-point coaching effect would yield about an 8 percentile improvement.

Given current admissions practices, it is unlikely that percentile improvements of these magnitudes would substantially influence admissions decisions, except perhaps for students whose scores are at the margins of admissibility to variously selective institutions at whatever level. Even here, other factors are likely to outweigh a few additional percentiles on the SAT, unless rigid cutting scores are mandated. Nor is it likely that such improvements in percentile rank—from 7 to 10, from 50 to 58, from 93 to 95—would dramatically alter student self-concepts and aspirations, although any improvements in performance or ability should be realistically capitalized upon in student guidance.

The outcome for a 30-point coaching effect is not radically different. The corresponding percentile changes are about 5 percentiles for initial scores 1.5 standard deviations below the mean (from 7 to 12), less than 12 percentiles for initial scores at the mean (from 50 to 62), and

3 percentiles for initial scores 1.5 standard deviations above the mean (93 to 96). In this case of a 30-point coaching effect, however, the percentile changes close to the mean, having exceeded a decile, are more noticeable and might have practical significance in selective instances. But coaching effects of these magnitudes, judging from the available research evidence, are not easily attainable, especially in Verbal (see Table 1). According to Figure 1, an expected 20-point SAT-V score effect would be associated with about 57 hours of contact time for motivated task-oriented students in a Verbal coaching program, while a 20-point SAT-M effect is associated with about 19 hours in a Math coaching program. An expected 30-point score effect would be associated with 260 hours for Verbal and 45 hours for Math. These score effects, of course, are average values expected to be associated with coaching programs of these durations, so some individuals would achieve variably larger gains with these amounts of contact time while other individuals would attain variably smaller gains. Moreover, given the possibility of interactions between score effects and various personal or background characteristics of the participants, certain groups or types of students might experience markedly higher or lower increases than that typified by the average score effect, but such interactions have not been well documented (Messick, 1980a).

As has already been suggested, any practical utility that coaching effects might convey is likely to be greatest for that subgroup of students whose uncoached scores are at the margins of admissibility to selective institutions of their choice, in whatever score ranges those institutions deem marginal. But it should be remembered that score increases attributable to coaching may arise in three possible ways, and although any one of them might move a student from inadmissible to admissible status in terms of test scores, they have different implications for subsequent college performance. These three types of coaching effects are schematized in Figure 2 in relation to admissible and inadmissible ranges of test scores and to successful and unsuccessful ranges of criterion performance.

Type A coaching effects in Figure 2 derive from enhanced test-taking sophistication or reduced test anxiety, by means of which uncoached scores that were inaccurately low because of construct-irrelevant test difficulty are raised to levels more accurately descriptive of student ability. Some students invalidly deemed inadmissible in terms of the formerly inaccurate scores might now be validly deemed admissible in terms of the more accurate assessment of ability levels. Type B coaching effects reflect genuine improvements in the comprehension and reasoning abilities measured by the SAT. Some students validly deemed inadmissible in terms of low prior ability levels might now be validly deemed

**Figure 2. Three Possible Coaching Effects
in Relation to College Performance**

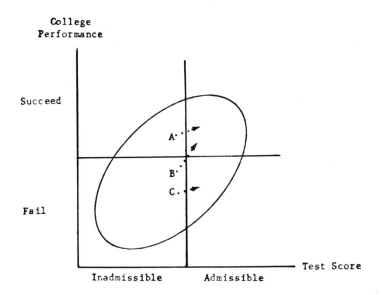

Source: Adapted from Hammond, 1980.

admissible by virtue of improved abilities sufficient for successful college performance. Type C coaching effects derive from test-taking stratagems and answer-selection tricks, resulting in increased test scores that are inaccurately high as assessments of student ability. As a consequence, some students validly deemed inadmissible in terms of the more accurate prior scores might now be invalidly deemed admissible by virtue of inaccurately high scores masking insufficiently high ability levels.

Students, especially those from diverse cultural backgrounds, stress type A effects; commercial coaching schools claim type B effects; and, professional testing organizations denigrate type C effects (Hammond, 1980). As we have seen, there may be a modicum of substance in all three positions, but the important point is that these potential effects are neither equally likely nor equally consequential. For example, types A and B, if realized, should enhance both student performance and test validity while type C should be only incidental with professionally made tests. To the extent that they occur, type A has implications for testing practice and type B for educational practice; both raise questions of equity of access to effective coaching programs, which is the next—and final—set of interrelated issues to be addressed.

Implications for Educational and Testing Practice. If coaching were to substantially increase test scores without correspondingly improving the abilities measured, there would be important implications for testing practice. Such an outcome would imply that the test or the testing experience entails unintended sources of difficulty that can be at least partially overcome by special preparation—anxiety over being evaluated, for instance, or unfamiliarity with item formats or test-taking strategies. In addition, effective coaching might reduce the operative difficulty level of some test items by teaching answer-selection tricks. As we have seen, the latter possibility is unlikely for professionally made tests, but to the extent that it does occur, the affected items should be revised or eliminated and the procedures for test development and analysis tightened. Although the former possibility—that enhanced test wiseness or anxiety reduction might lead to sizable score increases—is also unlikely to be of major consequence for the generality of students, it may be of special significance for certain groups or types of students such as test novices or those who are not culturally attuned to standardized testing. This suggests—even though the available studies find only small average effects, if any, associated with coaching programs stressing test familiarization and practice—that in the interest of equity all test candidates should have an opportunity to familiarize themselves with appropriate test formats and to practice recommended test-taking strategies. Such familiarization might be accomplished, for example, through the diligent use of practice tests and advisory materials similar to those routinely distributed by the College Board. Issues of equity of access to such test-wiseness coaching programs and materials become important mainly to the extent that individual differences in test-taking skills per se influence test scores.

On the other hand, if score increases attributable to coaching represent commensurate improvements in the verbal and mathematical abilities measured by the SAT, then there would be important implications for educational practice and social policy. To begin with, the functional characteristics of any SAT coaching programs that prove to be effective would have direct implications for instructional practice, for although there is little question that the comprehension and reasoning skills measured by the SAT are learned, there are large questions about how they can be taught. And if they *can* be taught, their status as explicit objectives of school learning must be addressed. Since comprehension and reasoning abilities facilitate educational accomplishments generally—the SAT is related, after all, not only to college performance but also to high school performance—school programs stressing ability development as well as subject-matter learning should have synergistic effects on current and subsequent educational achievement. In addition, as Cronbach and Snow (1977) insist, "the most important safeguard against rigidity of streaming is to make the development of aptitude a deliberate goal of instruction" (p. 521). All of this implies, assuming comprehension and reasoning skills are teachable, that the most efficacious approach to elementary and secondary education—as well as the soundest long-range mode of preparation for the SAT—would be school programs that integrate the development of thought with the development of knowledge.

If coaching techniques for fostering ability development could be specified that were not an integral part of the regular school experience, then the issue of equity of access to special coaching programs arises. The SAT measures the current level of developed scholastic abilities facilitative of academic learning. Whether this current level of developed abilities derives in part from special coaching programs pointed toward improved test performance or from general educational programs pointed toward improved school performance or from extensive experiential learning in nonschool settings—that is, from coaching or instruction or experience—is indistinguishable to the SAT. Thus, the issue of equity of access to coaching programs that are effective by virtue of ability development, if such could be identified, is similar to the issue of equity of access to effective school programs or effective life experiences, for they each have similar consequences for test scores. Such ability-enhancing coaching programs raise important equity issues of educational access, to be sure, but they are not new equity issues nor are they unique to coaching.

References

Alderman, D. L., and Powers, D. E. "The Effects of Special Preparation on SAT-Verbal Scores." *American Educational Research Journal*, 1980, *17*, 239–253. (Also reported as ETS RR 79-1 and CB RDR 78–79, No. 4. Princeton, N.J.: Educational Testing Service, 1979.)

Anastasi, A. "Abilities and the Measurement of Achievement." In W. B. Schrader (Ed.), *New Directions for Testing and Measurement: Measuring Achievement: Progress Over a Decade*, no. 5. San Francisco: Jossey-Bass, 1980.

Carroll, J. B. "On the Theory-Practice Interface in the Measurement of Intellectual Abilities." In P. Suppes (Ed.), *Impact of Research on Education: Some Case Studies*. Washington, D.C.: National Academy of Education, 1978.

Churchman, C. W. *The Design of Inquiring Systems: Basic Concepts of Systems and Organization.* New York: Basic Books, 1971.

Churchman, C. W. *The Systems Approach and Its Enemies.* New York: Basic Books, 1979.

Cochran, W. G. "The Use of Covariance in Observational Studies." *Applied Statistics,* 1968, *17,* 270–275.

Coffman, W. E., and Parry, M. E. "Effects of an Accelerated Reading Course on SAT-V Scores." *Personnel and Guidance Journal,* 1967, *46,* 292–296.

Cronbach, L. J. "Validity on Parole: How Can We Go Straight?" In W. B. Schrader (Ed.), *New Directions for Testing and Measurement: Measuring Achievement: Progress Over a Decade,* no. 5. San Francisco: Jossey-Bass, 1980.

Cronbach, L. J., and Snow, R. E. *Aptitudes and Instructional Methods.* New York: Wiley, 1977.

Dear, R. E. *The Effect of a Program of Intensive Coaching on SAT Scores* (ETS RB 58-5). Princeton, N.J.: Educational Testing Service, 1958. (Reported in French, J. W., and Dear, R. E. "Effect of Coaching on an Aptitude Test." *Educational and Psychological Measurement,* 1959, *19,* 319–330.)

Dyer, H. S. "Does Coaching Help?" *College Board Review,* 1953, *19,* 331–335. (Reported in French, J. W., and Dear, R. E. "Effect of Coaching on an Aptitude Test." *Educational and Psychological Measurement,* 1959, *19,* 319–330.)

English, H. B., and English, A. C. *A Comprehensive Dictionary of Psychological and Psychoanalytical Terms.* New York: Longman, 1958.

Evans, F. R., and Pike, L. W. "The Effects of Instruction for Three Mathematics Item Formats." *Journal of Educational Measurement,* 1973, *10,* 257–272.

Federal Trade Commission, Bureau of Consumer Protection. *Effects of Coaching on Standardized Admission: Revised Statistical Analyses of Data Gathered by Boston Regional Office of the Federal Trade Commission.* Washington, D.C.: Federal Trade Commission, Bureau of Consumer Protection, 1979.

Frankel, E. "Effects of Growth, Practice, and Coaching on Scholastic Aptitude Test Scores." *Personnel and Guidance Journal,* 1960, *38,* 713–719.

French, J. W. *The Coachability of the SAT in Public Schools* (ETS RB 55-26). Princeton, N.J.: Educational Testing Service, 1955. (Reported in French, J. W., and Dear, R. E. "Effect of Coaching on an Aptitude Test." *Educational and Psychological Measurement,* 1959, *19,* 319–330.)

Hammond, K. R. *Integrating Fact and Value in Discussions with Ralph Nader.* Colloquium presented at Educational Testing Service, Princeton, N.J., April 1980.

Kaplan, A. *The Conduct of Inquiry.* San Francisco: Chandler, 1964.

Marron, J. E. *Preparatory School Test Preparation: Special Test Preparation, Its Effect on College Board Scores and the Relationship of Affected Scores to Subsequent College Performance.* West Point, N.Y.: Research Division, Office of the Director of Admissions and Registrar, United States Military Academy, 1965.

Messick, S. "The Standard Problem: Meaning and Values in Measurement and Evaluation." *American Psychologist,* 1975, *30,* 955–966.

Messick, S. *The Effectiveness of Coaching for the SAT: Review and Reanalysis of Research From the Fifties to the FTC* (ETS RR 80-8). Princeton, N.J.: Educational Testing Service, 1980a.

Messick, S. "Test Validity and the Ethics of Assessment." *American Psychologist,* 1980b, *35,* 1012–1027.

Messick, S. "Constructs and Their Vicissitudes in Educational and Psychological Measurement." *Psychological Bulletin,* 1981a, *89,* 575–588.

Messick, S. *Evidence and Ethics in the Evaluation of Tests* (ETS RR 81-9). Princeton, N.J.: Educational Testing Service, 1981b (*Educational Researcher,* in press).

Messick, S., and Jungeblut, A. "Time and Method in Coaching for the SAT." *Psychological Bulletin,* 1981, *89,* 191–216.

Pallone, N. J. "Effects of Short-Term and Long-Term Developmental Reading Courses upon SAT Verbal Scores." *Personnel and Guidance Journal,* 1961, *39,* 654–657.

Pike, L. W. *Short-Term Instruction, Testwiseness and the Scholastic Aptitude Test: A Literature Review with Research Recommendations* (ETS RB 78-2 and CB RDR 77-78, No. 2). Princeton, N.J.: Educational Testing Service, 1978.

Roberts, S. O., and Oppenheim, D. B. *The Effect of Special Instruction upon Test Performance of High School Students in Tennessee* (ETS RB 66-36 and CB RDR 66-7, No. 1). Princeton, N.J.: Educational Testing Service, 1966.

Slack, W. V., and Porter, D. "The Scholastic Aptitude Test: A Critical Appraisal." *Harvard Educational Review,* 1980, *50,* 154–175.

Snow, R. E. "Representative and Quasi-Representative Designs for Research on Teaching." *Review of Educational Research,* 1974, *44,* 265–291.

Stallings, J. "Allocated Academic Learning Time Revisited, or Beyond Time on Task." *Educational Researcher,* 1980, *9* (11), 11–16.

Stroud, T. W. F. *Reanalysis of the Federal Trade Commission Study of Commercial Coaching for the SAT* (ETS RR 80-10). Princeton, N.J.: Educational Testing Service, 1980.

Webster's Seventh New Collegiate Dictionary. Springfield, Mass.: G. & C. Merriam, 1969.

Whitla, D. K. "Effect of Tutoring on Scholastic Aptitude Test Scores." *Personnel and Guidance Journal,* 1962, *41,* 32–37.

Samuel Messick is Distinguished Research Scientist and vice-president for research at the Educational Testing Service, Princeton, N.J., and adjunct professor of psychology at the Graduate School and University Center, City University of New York. He has been a fellow at the Institute for the Application of Mathematics in the Social Sciences, Stanford University, and a fellow at the Center for Advanced Study in the Behavioral Sciences. He has served as president of both the Psychometric Society and the Division of Evaluation and Measurement of the American Psychological Association.

*The existence or nonexistence of biases in mental testing is a
crucial scientific, social, and political issue. While some
forms of bias (for example, bias in selection and prediction)
appear amenable to definitional consensus, a definition of
cultural bias will remain problematic so long as it is
confused with the nature/nurture issue.*

Bias in Mental Tests

Lloyd Bond

By any standard, the problem of test bias is one of the most hotly debated topics in psychology and education. It pervades much of the controversy surrounding placement in classes for the educable mentally retarded, and it figures prominently in the often heard charge that tests systematically exclude large segments of the population from obtaining jobs, attending the elite schools, and entering prestigious professions such as medicine and the law. Moreover, test bias has led to widespread disenchantment with IQ tests. In this chapter I will discuss all of these issues, but first some preliminary remarks regarding conceptual issues are in order.

In the technical literature, and to a lesser extent in the public mind, two kinds of bias exist in tests. On the one hand, it is felt that the test as a whole is biased. That is, the total test score for members of one group (and hence the total test itself) either systematically underestimates the status of members of that group, or the test is simply inappropriate for the group. The alternative view is that many, if not most, of the items on a test are equally appropriate and accurate and measure the same construct across groups, but that individual items may be biased. This paper will deal primarily with the former definition, namely, total test bias.

B. F. Green (Ed.), *New Directions for Testing and Measurement: Issues in
Testing—Coaching, Disclosure, and Ethnic Bias,* no. 11. San Francisco:
Jossey-Bass, September 1981.

Few persons concerned about the problem of test bias or group differences in test performance would object to the statements that "test results indicate that white students, on the average, achieve higher levels of competence in most academic subjects than black students, on the average," or "males, as a group, achieve higher levels of competence in mathematics than females." The reason that the above statements are not viewed as prejudiced or racist remarks is that they are mere statements of fact. They are statements regarding past *achievement* in a given domain, irrespective of the reasons for any group differences present.

But, if we change the above statement slightly to read "test results indicate that white students as a group possess greater aptitude for academic work than black students as a group," or "males possess a greater aptitude for mathematics than females," the reaction is decidedly different. The latter statements raise the specter of "innateness" and therefore biological or genetic determinism. With the exception possibly of a few "radical" behaviorists, few persons nowadays believe that intellectual functioning, whether measured by tests or by one's intellectual achievements, is exclusively a function of either one's heredity or one's environment. Clearly, it is some complex function of both. Moreover, very little controversy arises if discussion is restricted to *individual* differences. It is when the issue is *group* differences in intellectual functioning that controversy arises.

In order to understand why the debate over test bias seems never ending and seems to become even more intense as more data are accumulated on the subject, it is necessary to start at the very beginning of the test construction process. What will we call our measure?

Ebel (1976) has stated that psychologists do not call a series of word problems, verbal analogies, vocabulary items, and spatial reasoning problems an "Academic Problems Test." They call it a test of "Mental Ability" or "General Intelligence." Similarly, a test that asks a series of commonly encountered social and practical problems is not labeled as such, but is called a test of "Practical Judgment" and is used to support rather tenuous theories of social interaction. Flaugher (1978) notes that it is a great leap of faith to declare that someone who does not answer enough such items with the keyed responses is "lacking in practical judgment."

The reason for the broad labeling of the test is the need for more general constructs than is implied when one labels a test a "problems" test. Constructs are the building blocks of a science. A science advances precisely to the extent that its constructs are accurately measured and their interrelationships are sufficiently well known to explain observable phenomena. The constructs of weight, mass, force, momentum, and volume in physics can be measured precisely, and their interrelationship can be accurately specified.

Psychology, on the other hand, is plagued not only by less precise measurement but also by considerably less agreement as to the very nature of its constructs and their interrelationships. Many psychologists trained in test theory, for example, consider the first principal component of a component analysis of many tests as an ideal operationalization (some would say a definition) of intelligence (Jensen, 1980). By first principal component I mean that hypothetical, underlying variable that causes most tests of mental ability to be positively correlated. But other psychologists and many lay persons find this definition wanting. The concept "intelligence" carries enormous surplus meaning in the public mind. To many people, creativity and business acumen, for example, are clearly instances of "intelligence" and if IQ tests correlate with these attributes only modestly (around 0.5) then that is the fault of too narrow a conceptualization and measurement of intelligence. In a very real sense, this criticism is on the mark. Psychologists are wont to begin their discussions of intelligence with a disclaimer that presents a narrow, operationalized definition of intelligence. But once the definition is given, it is quickly forgotten, and in later discussion the term intelligence is used in a manner that is indistinguishable from the rich meaning it has in everyday discourse.

There are essentially three ways in which a test may be biased against a given individual or group of individuals. First, a test may be biased on the basis of strictly internal criteria. That is, the test is judged to be biased on the basis of the very items that comprise it. A verbal analogies test, for example, might contain words that tend to favor one group over another. A test that purports to measure intelligence may contain words to which some group or groups have been exposed more than others. This is in fact the major charge against IQ tests with respect to blacks.

A second possible source of bias emanates from a wide variety of situational factors that are essentially external to the test itself. These include such factors as race, sex, language, and attitude of the examiner; test anxiety, achievement motivation, and self-esteem of examinees; and some more closely test-related factors such as speed and timing of the test and the actual format (multiple choice versus open ended) of the test items.

The third possible source of bias comes from the use of tests in employment and college admissions. The literature on this type of bias has increased tremendously over the past ten years, and, it turns out, the issue of selection and prediction is far more complex than was initially

supposed. We will discuss in detail various models of selection and prediction bias. For the moment, it is sufficient to note that the fundamental
definition of bias of this type is that it exists when the same test score
predicts different levels of job or scholastic performance for different
groups.

Construct and Content Bias

Suppose a teacher wished to assess the verbal analogical reasoning
of her eighth grade class and constructed an analogies test that contained terms familiar to rural students, say, but relatively unfamiliar to
urban students. A typical item on the test might be:

pig:sty::chicken: _____

(a) barn (b) table (c) turkey (d) coop (e) dinner

It should be obvious that students raised on a farm would be at a tremendous advantage over urban students on such a test. Rural students
as a group would probably score significantly better on the test than
urban students. The reason for this, of course, is that rural students are
more likely than urban students to know the meanings of the words in
the given analogy. The test is a much more veridical measure of *analogical reasoning* for rural students. The typical urban student is penalized
because of his unfamiliarity with the very words which make up the
analogy. For the urban student, the test is as much a test of vocabulary as
it is one of analogical reasoning. This example illustrates what is known
as *construct bias*. Construct bias exists whenever a test purporting to measure a single construct in fact measures different constructs in different
groups. In the above example, rural students are likely to be quite
homogeneous with respect to their exposure to and familiarity with the
words on the test. The test is therefore a "purer" measure of verbal
reasoning for them. It is uncontaminated by large differences in vocabulary. For urban students, their ranking on the analogies test reflects
(to a much greater extent than rural students) their ranking on the
conceptually unrelated construct, vocabulary.

Parenthetically, it should be pointed out that, as a practical measurement matter, it is impossible to separate "vocabulary" from "verbal
analogical reasoning." But conceptually they are different. Although
there is no way to avoid this problem when constructing a test, there are
ways to control statistically for differences in such unwanted variables.
The procedure involves giving a separate test of vocabulary; then com-

paring only those students on the analogies test who have the same vocabulary scores.

The important point to note is that the only valid comparisons are those among rural students. Any other comparisons are suspect. Inferring that student A (a rural student) is better in verbal reasoning than student B (an urban student) is obviously confounded by vocabulary differences. Comparing two urban students, although a clearly less egregious error, is still problematical because the extent of individual differences in knowledge of rural terms is likely to be much larger in this group.

The above illustration exemplifies the charge made by most critics of IQ tests who claim that such tests draw upon language, terms, expressions, and values familiar to white, middle-class America, but relatively unfamiliar to blacks, Hispanics, and other distinct cultural groups. Determining whether this is in fact so has produced a tremendous amount of empirical data (Jensen, 1980). Despite this, opposing points of view seem to have hardened rather than come together. Part of the reason for this rigidity of positions on the matter is the subtle merging, in the minds of both psychologists and the public, of two related but fundamentally different issues—the existence or nonexistence of bias on the one hand and the nature-nurture controversy on the other. We will return to this point later.

The most comprehensive, yet still incomplete, psychometric analyses and review of construct and content bias in mental tests undertaken to date is that of Jensen (1980). He discusses a series of criteria for test bias that have been investigated by researchers. These include, among other things: (1) differences in performance across groups on verbal versus nonverbal items and on items judged to be "most culturally loaded" versus items judged to be "least culturally loaded," (2) factor analysis of mental ability tests for various cultural groups (primarily blacks and whites), (3) examination of the reliabilities of mental tests across groups, and, finally, (4) correlations between item difficulties across groups.

Verbal Versus Nonverbal Items. It should be obvious that it is impossible to measure intelligence, however defined, without at the same time measuring one's exposure to the symbols in the test to which the examinee must respond. In fact, a fundamental and necessary assumption in measures of "aptitude" is that experience with and exposure to the content of the test is a constant for all individuals (Donlon and Angoff, 1971). Yet, it still seems reasonable to suppose that verbal tests would be more susceptible to cultural biases than nonverbal tests. Nonverbal tests contain items that have geometrical figures, abstract matrices, and other nonverbal stimuli. With respect to black-white differences on mental tests, a plausible hypothesis is that blacks would be at a greater disadvantage on verbal as opposed to nonverbal items. The variety of ways that cultural or experiential factors can influence test performance seems much greater for verbal items, where specific language usage would be more relevant.

Jensen (1980), McGurk (1975), and Roberts (1971), among others, have reviewed the literature on this topic for large samples of black and white students on numerous individual and group tests. The general finding is that either the black-white differences in performance on the two types of items is the same or is in fact larger on nonverbal items. For example, Roberts (1971) found in a sample of approximately 1,000 students (of whom 14 percent were black) that the two groups differed by 0.78 of a standard deviation on the vocabulary subtest of the WISC and 0.76 of a standard deviation on the block design subtest. McGurk (1975), reviewing some 80 studies conducted between 1950 and 1970 found that slightly over 19 percent of the black students exceeded the white median on nonverbal items, while only 15 percent exceeded the white median scores on verbal items. If cultural and experiential factors play a part in black-white differences on mental tests, they apparently do so in ways that are much more complex than the simple verbal/nonverbal distinction would imply.

The verbal/nonverbal dichotomy is similar to the division of items into the categories "most culturally loaded" and "least culturally loaded." The enormously complex ways in which culture may affect cognitive functioning seems to have dissuaded neither researchers nor the courts from the belief that by simply inspecting an item one could tell how and in what ways the item favored certain groups. There are some obvious cases where this is possible (as with the rural-urban example earlier) but beyond these, this approach to test bias does not appear promising. In general, black-white and male-female differences in test performance do not vary as a function of items judged by "experts" to be culturally loaded or sexist (compare McGurk, 1953 and Fox, 1976).

Factor Analysis. Factor analysis is a statistical procedure for reducing a large number of mental ability tests to a much smaller number of underlying or primary dimensions. For example, Thurstone (1935), a pioneer in the history of factor analysis and mental ability measurement, posited seven basic mental abilities (verbal comprehension, word fluency, numerical ability, spatial ability, associative memory, perceptual speed, and induction). Factor analyses of numerous mental ability measures for various groups, including blacks, normally result in five to seven factors that closely resemble the above dimensions (Jensen, 1980; Anastasi, 1976). The most widely used standardized tests do appear to measure similar constructs in various subpopulations of society. It should not be concluded, however, that there are only seven "mental abilities." Indeed, Guilford (1967) has proposed some 120 abilities, but progress toward developing measures of each ability has been slow.

Reliability. A weak criterion for test bias is that the test is equally reliable for all groups. The reliability of a test refers to the accuracy or repeatability of the scores one obtains. If a test measures the same construct in two different groups, then it should measure that construct with comparable accuracy. Most cognitive ability tests exhibit comparable reliabilities across diverse groups (including linguistic, cultural, and ethnic minorities). The reason reliability, per se, is a weak criterion for establishing bias is that the test may measure essentially different attributes in two populations with equal accuracy. To take an extreme example, cognitive ability tests that are written in English have been found to be equally reliable for both Hispanics, many of whom speak English as a second language, and native English speakers. Yet, it should be obvious that knowledge of English and the cognitive ability being measured are both reflected in the scores of Hispanic persons. Each of these attributes may be measured reliably. Comparable reliability across groups is a necessary, but not sufficient, condition for the nonexistence of bias.

Correlations Between Item Difficulties Across Groups. The rationale for examining the rank order of item difficulties across groups as a possible indication of bias is that items should "behave" in the same way for two or more groups if the same trait is being measured. Stated differently, all of the items should measure what one is interested in measuring in more or less the same manner, and hence, easy items for one group should be easy items for another, and difficult items for one group should be difficult items for the other. If the correlation between item difficulties (that is, the proportion of persons getting the item correct) across two groups is high, above 0.90 say, then it can be argued that in a statistical and psychometric sense, the same or a similar trait is being measured in both groups.

Jensen (1980), Miele (1979), Nichols (1972), and Kennedy and others (1963), as well as other researchers, have compared cross-racial correlations of item difficulties on the Wechsler Intelligence Scale for Children (WISC) and the Stanford-Binet for large samples of blacks and whites. In all cases, a ranking of item difficulties in the white samples closely paralleled the ranking in the black sample. Pearson product-moment correlations were uniformly above 0.90 and in one instance (Kennedy and others, 1963) was 0.99.

High cross-racial correlations of item difficulties or, equivalently, the absence of group times item interactions in an analysis of variance of an items times subjects times groups matrix (see Shepard, this volume) is *consistent* with the hypothesis of no construct bias. It, of course, does not prove the absence of bias. According to Jensen (1980) and Gordon and Rudert (1979), however, a similar analysis involving correlations *within* race, across age and ability levels, all but destroys any serious counter-argument that tests are biased in the construct and content sense.

Responding to the charge that IQ and other mental ability tests are biased against blacks in the sense that they may measure "intelligence" in whites but measure "access to information" in blacks, the above investigators considered the correlations of item difficulties between low and high scoring individuals within each race and the correlations of item difficulties between age groups within each race. As it turns out, items that discriminate most between whites and blacks are essentially the same items that discriminate most between older and younger children within each race and, moreover, are the same items that discriminate most between high and low scoring individuals of the same age within each race. Gordon and Rudert (1979) give the following summary of their major conclusion:

> The absence of race-by-item interaction in all of these studies places severe constraints on models of the test score difference between the races that rely on differential access to information. . . . Items of information must . . . pass over the racial boundary at all times and places in order of their level of difficulty among whites, which means that they must diffuse across race in exactly the same order in which they diffuse across age boundaries, from older to younger, among both whites and blacks. These requirements imply that diffusion across race also mimics exactly the diffusion of information from brighter to slower youngsters of the same age within each group. Even if one postulates a vague but broad kind of experience that behaves in exactly this manner, it should be evident that it would represent but a thinly disguised tautology for the mental functions that IQ tests are designed to measure (pp. 179–180).

The sheer bulk and consistency of the above analyses of content and construct bias are persuasive. Indeed, if psychometric and statistical analyses were the only kinds of evidence available, then such evidence would be overwhelmingly in favor of the conclusion that biases internal to IQ tests are nonexistent with respect to blacks and whites. Even if the question of what IQ tests "really" measure is ignored, the above analyses clearly demonstrate that the *structure* and *pattern* of the attributes measured are remarkably similar. Thus, if differential cultural experiences do produce the consistent mean score difference among blacks and whites on IQ tests (as the study to be described later suggests), these same differential experiences have *not* altered the basic structure and pattern of cognitive functioning.

Bias and the IQ Controversy. One reason that bias (in the construct and content sense of the term) is so persistent and so volatile an issue is that it seems to imply something regarding the controversy surrounding race differences in intelligence. That is to say, many people, including many psychologists, apparently believe that if a test of intelligence is shown to be free of content and construct bias, then there is strong evidence for the notion that mean differences on such tests have a substantial genetic component. This is a complicated and profoundly misguided notion. The demonstration that a test is measuring essentially similar attributes in two groups has no a priori implication for the *source* of any group differences which emerge. To understand just why the merging of the bias question and the IQ controversy is misguided, we will have to move beyond internal analyses of tests and look instead at broader questions concerning cultural and early childhood experiences.

In a classic study of adoption of black infants by advantaged white families in Minnesota, Scarr and Weinberg (1976) have provided the most intriguing and compelling data so far gathered on the effects of cross-racial adoption on the IQ scores of black children. These investigators located 101 advantaged white families in Minnesota who had adopted 130 black or interracial infants. The natural parents of the adopted infants were indistinguishable educationally from their age cohorts in the general population. Actually, the black mothers of the adopted infants had one year less education, 10.8 years, than black females in their age group (25–44).

The 130 adopted children were tested between the ages of four and seven with the Wechsler Intelligence Scale for Children (WISC). The mean of their IQ scores was 106, 6 points above the national white average, 21 points above the typical 85 for blacks, and 16 points above blacks reared in the same geographical area. The children were similarly above average on school-administered achievement and aptitude tests. This study illustrates perhaps more than any other that IQ scores are quite malleable. Moreover, the study indicates that, in ways not yet completely understood, the skills that IQ tests measure reflect practices, values, attitudes, skills, and patterns of parent-child interaction (an entire ecological system) of white, middle-class families. The Scarr-Weinberg study calls into question the widespread and conceptually naive practice of "controlling" for social-class differences between blacks and whites, and thereby presuming that differences in IQ relevant variables have been completely removed.

The results of this classic study simply are inconsistent with genetic explanations of race differences in IQ scores. If black children have biologically and genetically limited intellectual capacity, as some have claimed (Jensen, 1973; Shockley, 1971, 1972), their IQ performance should fall below that of other children adopted into advantaged white families. As Scarr and Weinberg note, however, the norm and range of reaction for black adoptees are indistinguishable from those of white adoptees. Norm and range of reaction refer to the fact that genotypes do not specify a single phenotype, but rather, they specify both a norm and a range of phenotypic responses that organisms can make to a wide variety of environmental conditions.

Biases External to the Test

Sources of bias that are external to the test itself include (1) differences in personality factors of persons taking the test such as differences in motivation, test-taking attitude, test anxiety, and self-esteem, (2) test sophistication, that is, the effects of prior test-taking experience and "coaching," and (3) the ethnic background, dialect, and sex of the person administering the test.

Personality Factors. Factors such as test anxiety (Matarazzo, 1972; Sarason, 1978), self-esteem (Shuey, 1978), and achievement motivation (Chapman and Hill, 1971; Banks and others, 1978) have been cited frequently as possible explanations for group differences in mental test performance. Common sense would suggest that these attributes are certainly related to "achievement" (for example, grades) if not to "intelligence." The research evidence, however, is rather meager.

Regarding test anxiety, the general finding is that *extreme* forms of anxiety affect all performances, including test performance (Anastasi, 1976), but there appears to be no basis for presuming that groups such as social classes, races, or the sexes differ markedly on this variable (see Noble, 1969 and Solkoff, 1972).

Surprisingly, since it is often presumed that self-esteem is a crucial variable in test performance, there is little evidence pro or con for this hypothesis. Clark (1965) and Shuey (1978) have demonstrated that blacks have lower self-esteem than whites, but this finding has not been systematically related to test scores in the samples studied.

Achievement motivation has been extensively studied, especially its relationship to academic grades (Atkinson and others, 1976), where the correlation is moderately positive. But its relationship to IQ scores has been found to be inconsistent (Chapman and Hill, 1971).

Test Sophistication, Practice, and Coaching. A sound and valid measure of some cognitive skill or ability should not, as mentioned earlier, be confounded with unrelated and unwanted variables. Thus, in mental tests, the purpose is to measure specific abilities such as vocabulary and reading comprehension, *not* unwanted variables such as the extent of prior practice with tests, the degree of "test-wiseness," or differences in guessing strategies. To the extent that test scores reflect these unwanted variables, interpretations of score differences as differences only in the construct presumably being measured are inaccurate.

The evidence on the effects of prior test-taking experience, test-wiseness, and coaching comes in two forms. First, there is the general question of whether differences in these characteristics are related to differences in test scores. Second, if such differences are related to test performance, do social classes, races, sexes, and other groups of interest differ significantly in these characteristics?

Several generalizations emerge from experimental tests of the first hypothesis (compare Vernon, 1960; James, 1953; Yates, 1953). In general, (1) practice effects are greatest for naive test takers who have had minimal experience with tests, (2) gains from practice on various forms of a test follow a law of diminishing returns, that is, initially, practice results in significant test increases, about 5 IQ points on the average (Jensen, 1980), but further practice and exposure show smaller and smaller effects (see also Messick, this volume), (3) verbal tests are generally less affected by practice and test familiarity than are nonverbal tests, and (4) the effects of practice are not ephemeral, but, rather, tend to be maintained upon repeated testing.

Recently there has been much debate over the effects of specifically coaching students in order to increase their performance on standardized tests, especially the SAT (Slack and Porter, 1980a, 1980b; Jackson, 1980; Messick, this volume). The coaching controversy is a socially important one because if commercial coaching schools are effective in raising test scores, then economically advantaged students, who can afford such schools, have yet another advantage over their less fortunately situated cohorts.

Unfortunately, much of the research in this area is of less than optimal quality. Many studies lack a carefully chosen control group of students who do not participate in the coaching sessions. Moreover, those studies with adequate controls rarely describe the coaching in sufficient detail for the reader to ascertain their instructional content. Consequently, coaching has come to mean everything from brief sessions of no more than a couple of hours consisting of test-wiseness hints such as "do easy items first," or "guess if you can eliminate one alternative" to sustained, quality instruction in the domain to be tested.

Messick (this volume) has critically reviewed the literature on coaching and has concluded that the methodologically sound studies show average increases (over what would be expected from normal growth and instruction in school) range from 10 to 15 points.

The interaction of race with practice and coaching has generated inconsistent results. Baughman and Dahlstrom (1968), Costello (1970) and Dyer (1970) concluded from experimental studies that employed general group mental ability tests that special practice for black students was no more effective than for whites. Messick (1980), however, in an analysis of data collected by the Federal Trade Commission, reported gains made by coached black students were substantially and significantly higher than for whites. The average coaching effect for the white students (n = 132) was −.25 on the 800 point SAT scale, while that for the black students (n = 13) was 46.5. Although this is a small sample, the difference of 47 points is quite substantial. Clearly, more research on this topic is needed.

The Effects of Examiner Characteristics. Considerable investigative energy has been devoted to detecting possible sources of bias in the person or persons administering mental tests, especially individually administered tests where verbal interaction and communication between the examiner and the examinees is maximum. The hypothesis of such investigations is that either the race and/or the dialect of the examiner would differentially affect the performance of some individuals. Many blacks, for example, speak a nonstandard dialect that is different from the language of the test examiner. Would scores for such youngsters on IQ and other mental ability tests increase substantially if the examiner spoke the dialect of the child during the test administration? Does the race or sex of the examiner interact with the race or sex of the examinee?

To date there have been thirty studies investigating the interaction of the race of examiner and the race of examinee. These have been classified by Jensen (1980) as having either (1) inadequate designs, (2) adequate but incomplete designs, or (3) adequate and complete designs depending, respectively, on whether they contained randomized assignment of at least two examiners of different races to examinees of both races, contained examinees from both races, or contained randomized assignment of examiners of both races to examinees of both races.

In the sixteen methodologically sound studies, ten revealed no significant differences in the performance of black (or white) subjects as a function of the race of the examiner. In the remaining six studies, small or inconsistent interactions between examiner race and examinee race were found. Although no strong inferences can be drawn from methodologically unsound studies, even these showed rather inconsistent and contradictory results. It can safely be concluded that the performance of minority children on IQ tests in current use is essentially unrelated to the race of the person administering the test.

Much less data exist on other characteristics of examiners that may differentially affect test performance. Of those characteristics that have been studied, neither sex (compare Rumenik and others, 1977) nor dialect (Quay, 1971, 1972, 1974) of the examiner appear to be related to race or sex differences in test scores.

Bias in Selection and Prediction

Of all of the possible forms test bias can take, one would think that selection and prediction bias would be the least controversial since, presumably, it is a straightforward statistical question whether a test predicts subsequent performance (in school or on the job) equally well for two groups. It turns out, however, that ascertaining whether a test is biased in the selection and prediction sense is at least as complicated as determining other forms of bias.

Selection and prediction bias has received enormous attention recently from psychometricians and mathematical psychologists (Cleary, 1968; Darlington, 1971; Einhorn and Bass, 1971; Thorndike, 1971a; Cole, 1973; Gross, 1975; Hunter and Schmidt, 1976; Novick and Petersen, 1976; Petersen and Novick, 1976). An entire issue of the *Journal of Education Measurement* has in fact been devoted to the single topic of bias in selection.

We will first consider several mathematical models of bias in selection and prediction and will then review briefly the empirical data on bias in the prediction of academic work and in employment settings. Petersen and Novick (1976) have provided the most comprehensive and penetrating review of the various bias models. My terminology follows theirs closely.

The Regression Model. According to Cleary (1968):

> A test is biased for members of a subgroup of the population if, in the prediction of the criterion for which the test was designed, consistent nonzero errors of prediction are made for members of the subgroup. In other words, the test is biased if the criterion score predicted from the common regression line is consistently too high or too low for members of the subgroup. With this definition of bias, there may be a connotation of "unfair," particularly if the use of the test produces a prediction that is too low (p. 115).

This definition of test bias is called the regression model because in practical situations the existence of bias is determined by examining the least-squares linear regression lines for two different groups. If the regression lines differ in either their slopes, intercepts, or both, then the test is biased according to this definition. Figure 1 illustrates this point with four of many possible situations. Figure 1a is an example of *intercept bias.* The *slopes* of the regression lines are identical. But, for a given test score, the criterion performance for members of group 1 is systematically higher than that for group 2. Under this model, then, the test is biased against members of group 1 since many in this group who would

Figure 1. Examples of Selection Bias According to the Regression Model

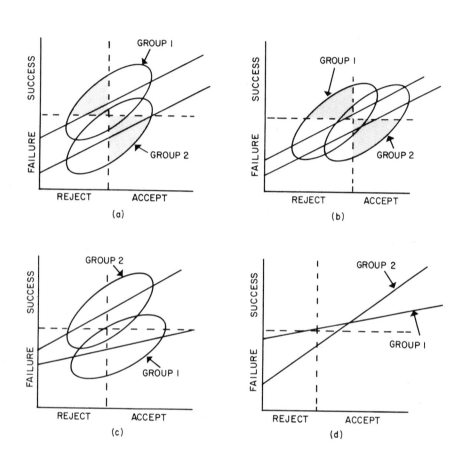

have been successful are rejected in favor of many members of group 2 who in fact were unsuccessful. The test does not distinguish between the two groups (that is, their mean and variance are approximately equal), yet the groups differ significantly on the criterion.

In Figure 1b, the opposite occurs. The groups are indistinguishable on the criterion, but differ significantly on the test. Thus, two individuals, one in group 1 and the other in group 2, who perform identically on the criterion, have significantly different test scores. The test is biased against members of group 1. Members in the shaded portion of group 1, who would have been successful, are rejected in favor of members in the shaded portion of group 2, who were in fact unsuccessful. In both of these cases, use of the combined regression line or use of the group 2 regression would result in a test that is biased against group 1.

Figures 1c and 1d are examples of *slope bias* in the regression model. In Figure 1c, the regression lines intersect outside the range of possible test scores. In Figure 1d, they intersect within the range of possible test scores. The implication of these two conditions is that in the former case, use of the group 2 (or combined) regression line results in systematically increasing overprediction of group 1 performance. The test is therefore biased against group 2. Members of this group who would have been successful are rejected in favor of unsuccessful members of group 1.

The situation depicted in Figure 1d is more complicated. Here, use of the group 2 (or combined) regression line systematically *overpredicts* group 1 performance to the right of the intersection point, in some instances, and systematically *underpredicts* group 1 performance to the left of the intersection. It should be obvious that in this situation the actual extent of unfairness to any particular member of a group depends crucially on the test cutoff score. If the cutoff score is to the right of the intersection of the regression lines, the test is always biased in favor of group 1. If the cutoff score is to the left of the intersection point, in some instances, the test is biased in favor of low-scoring individuals in group 2.

The Constant Ratio Model. Thorndike (1971a) makes the useful distinction between a test that may be fair to *individuals* in a given group but unfair to the group as a whole. As stated before, in the Cleary model, a test is fair if both the slope and the intercept of the regression lines for two subpopulations are equal. The practical implication is that two individual applicants from two different groups who have the same test score will have the same probability of being selected. Thorndike demonstrates, however, that even if a test has equal regression lines for two groups, if the difference between the groups on the test varies from the difference between the two groups on the criterion, then the test may be considered fair to individuals within each group, but unfair to the group as a whole. The reason for this is that the proportion of those in the lower scoring group who meet some minimum acceptable score on the test will be smaller, relative to the high-scoring group, than the proportion that will reach a specified level of criterion performance. Thus, Thorndike proposed the following definition of a fair selection test: "The qualifying scores on a test should be set at levels that will qualify applicants in two groups in proportion to the fraction of the two groups reaching a specified level of criterion performance" (p. 63).

Petersen and Novick (1976) call the Thorndike model a constant ratio model because Thorndike's definition asserts that a test is fair if applicants are selected so that the ratio of the proportion selected to the proportion successful is the same for all groups.

Cole (1973) has noted that the Thorndike model of fair selection can be represented formally as follows: Given a minimum level of satisfactory performance, (y'), on the criterion, a selection test is fair if for any two subpopulations 1 and 2,

$$\frac{\text{Prob }(X \geq x_1)}{\text{Prob }(Y \geq y')} = \frac{\text{Prob }(X \geq x_2)}{\text{Prob }(Y \geq y')}$$

In the above equation X and Y are the score and criterion performance of a given individual and x_1 and x_2 are the cutoff scores on the test for subpopulations 1 and 2.

The Conditional Probability Model. Cole (1973) has proposed a model of fair selection which assures to any individual, regardless of his group membership, an equal chance of being selected, provided that he or she would have been successful if selected. According to Cole: The basic principle of the conditional probability selection model is that for both minority and majority groups whose members can achieve a satisfactory criterion score [Y ≥ y'] there should be the same probability of selection regardless of group membership (p. 240).

The Cole model of fair selection can be represented symbolically as follows

$$\text{Prob }(X \geq x_1 \mid Y \geq y') = \text{Prob }(X \geq x_2 \mid Y \geq y')$$

The notation Prob (A|B) is read "the probability of A given B," that is, the conditional probability of A. The above equation says that, given a fixed, minimum level of criterion performance (a certain grade point average, a certain number of parts produced per hour, and so forth), members of any two groups 1 and 2 who would be "successful" on the criterion should have the same probability of being selected. The practical implication is that a single cutoff score on the test for all groups may be unfair to certain groups under this approach. The cutoff score for each group must be set such that the probability of its potentially successful members being selected should be identical to other groups.

By way of review, it should be noted that in the Thorndike and Cole models of fair selection, two individuals with the same score on the selection tests could have unequal probabilities of selection. This situation is impossible under the Cleary, or classical, model. Both the Cole and Thorndike models are attractive because they advance a socially desirable end. In many situations, minorities, especially blacks, have lower mean scores on the criterion than whites, but this difference is less than the difference between blacks and whites on the test. The two selection models will almost always select minority applicants who do less well on the criterion, on the average, than majority applicants.

The Equal Probability Model. Linn (1973) describes a model which, following Petersen and Novick (1976), I will call the equal probability model. The model starts with the very reasonable assumption that what is "given" or known in practice is not an individual's future performance on the criterion, but rather his or her performance on the predictor test. The model thus argues that the conditional probability model described earlier should be reversed. That is, to be fair, the following equality must hold for any two groups 1 and 2:

$$\text{Prob } (Y \geqslant y' \mid X \geqslant x_1) = \text{Prob } (Y \geqslant y' \mid X \geqslant x_2)$$

where the terms are as defined earlier. Thus, the equal probability model requires that within the selected group for any subpopulation of applicants, the proportion of successful persons should be the same.

Associated with each of the above four models is a different index, which must be constant across all groups and which seems fair and plausible. Yet, in most situations they all result in different proportions of individuals being selected from the various subpopulations. Under such circumstances, how does one proceed? Petersen and Novick (1976) have provided a partial answer.

Converse Models. Petersen and Novick question all of the earlier models of fair selection, except the classical or Cleary Model, because their "converses" contain a contradiction. That is to say, the above models focus attention on those applicants who are selected and those who would be successful. The issue of fairness is discussed in relation to these individuals only. But questions of fairness can also be asked in relation to applicants who were either *not* selected or who would have been *unsuccessful* if selected. It turns out that when questions are phrased with these individuals in mind, the above models are internally inconsistent. For example, in the conditional probability model of fair selection, one can argue that potential *failures* should be rejected in no greater percentage in any group. Thus

$$\text{Prob}\ (X < x_1 \mid Y < y') = \text{Prob}\ (X < x_2 \mid Y < y')$$

is a constant for any two groups 1 and 2. With some straightforward algebraic manipulations, Petersen and Novick demonstrate that achieving fairness according to this definition (that is, being fair to potential failures) will be incompatible with being fair to potentially successful applicants in all but the most unusual set of circumstances. Similar internal inconsistencies occur in the converse constant ratio and converse equal probability models. Figure 2 illustrates the six equally reasonable models of fair selection and the implied ratio which must be equal across groups. For example, in the constant ratio model, the ratio of those who are accepted, VA + FA, to all those who were potentially successful, VA + FR, must be constant for all groups. Similarly, for the equal probability model, the ratio of the valid acceptances, VA, to the total acceptance, VA + FA, must be constant for all groups.

The above is by no means a complete discussion. Fair selection models have been proposed that take into account the probability of success, given a specific test score (Einhorn and Bass, 1971), while others (Jensen, 1980) adjust for unreliability in the test. It should be obvious, nevertheless, that issues of bias will not be settled by mathematical and methodological specialists. It is hoped, however, that serious discussions by such specialists will inform the courts and the public, who ultimately will decide such issues. Toward this end, Linn (1973), Petersen and Novick (1976) and Novick and Petersen (1976) have suggested that the question of *values* (in their terminology, "utilities") be made explicit in a model. Thus, we should attach an agreed upon and quantifiable weight to certain desired outcomes (for example, having minority police officers on the police force, having minority and female doctors, lawyers, and so on), and these value considerations should be as much a part of the criterion as objectively measured criterion performance.

Empirical Data on Bias in Prediction and Selection. None of the models of fair selection discussed here has been systematically investigated with real data. Cole (1973), in a simulation of several situations encountered in actual practice, has demonstrated that the models result in substantially different percentages of both minority and majority individuals being selected, given the same set of selection conditions.

In actual practice, only two types of validity studies comparing various groups, primarily blacks and whites, have been undertaken: studies of differential predictive validity and regression studies.

Figure 2. Comparison of Six Fair Selection Models

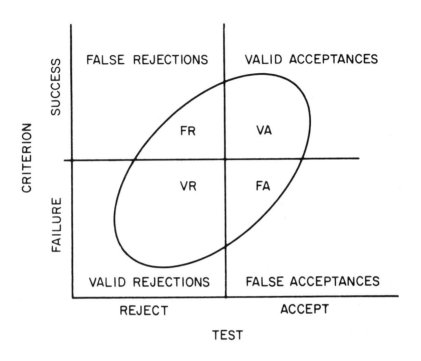

MODEL	RATIO
CONSTANT RATIO	(VA + FA) / (VA + FR)
CONDITIONAL PROBABILITY	VA / (VA + FR)
EQUAL PROBABILITY	VA / (VA + FA)
CONVERSE CONSTANT RATIO	(VR + FR)(VR + FA)
CONVERSE CONDITIONAL PROBABILITY	VR / (VR + FA)
CONVERSE EQUAL PROBABILITY	VR / (VR + FR)

Differential Predictive Validity. Differential predictive validity exists whenever the correlation between test scores and the performance the test is intended to predict differ significantly for two or more groups. Many believe, for example, that IQ tests and standardized aptitude tests, while valid predictors of school performance for white students, are either invalid for blacks (that is, the correlation is zero) or the correlation is significantly lower. A steadily accumulating body of evidence suggests that this is not as severe a source of bias as was initially supposed, either in the primary grades (Sattler, 1974), secondary schools (Boney, 1977), or college (Stanley and Porter, 1967; Stanley, 1971). Scholastic aptitude tests predict about equally well for both blacks and whites. This general finding does not appear to hold for the sexes, however, where a consistent finding is that predictive validities for females is somewhat higher than for males (Stanley, 1967).

In employment testing, the picture is less clear because the usual criterion in this situation, supervisory ratings, may be less reliable and may in fact be biased itself. Where objective criteria such as job knowledge are available, again the evidence seems to point to the conclusion that validities obtained for black employees are quite similar to those for whites (Campbell and others, 1973).

Regression Studies. A repeated finding from regression studies of test bias that has intrigued and surprised many is that when bias *is* detected in the prediction of blacks' criterion performance, especially academic performance, it is more often than not the case that *intercept bias* as distinct from *slope bias* is present, with the white intercept being higher than the black. This implies that the criterion performance of black students tends to be overpredicted if one uses the white or combined regression line. This of course is just the opposite of what is generally thought to be the case. A major criticism of tests is that they underpredict the performance of blacks. No empirically substantiated explanation of this unexpected result has been adduced.

Concluding Remarks

The presence or absence of bias in mental testing is an important scientific, social, and political question. In the current public debate, the problems in terminology and test labels render rational public discussion problematical. Yet, answers to questions involving bias in selection and prediction and, to a lesser extent, bias in factors external to the test, seem amenable to scientific if not social consensus. Public and scientific consensus on the existence of cultural, that is construct and content bias, however, seems a long way off. Construct and content bias has unfortunately been merged in the minds of many with the unrelated issue of

75

genetic versus environmental explanations of racial, ethnic, and social class differences in intelligence. There is one point, nevertheless, which seems to be universally agreed upon, and that is that the need for accurate, unbiased assessment in a democratic society is necessary and beneficial to all.

References

Anastasi, A. *Psychological Testing*. New York: MacMillan, 1976.
Atkinson, J. W., Lens, W., and O'Malley, P. M. "Motivation and Ability: Interactive Psychological Determinants of Intellective Performance, Educational Achievement, and Each Other." In W. H. Sewell, R. M. Hauser, and D. L. Featherman (Eds.), *Schooling and Achievement in American Society*. New York: Academic Press, 1976.
Banks, W. C., McQuater, G. V., and Hubbard, J. L. "Toward a Reconceptualization of the Social-Cognitive Bases of Achievement Orientations in Blacks." *Review of Educational Research*, 1978, *48* (3), 381–397.
Baughman, E. E., and Dahlstrom, W. G. *Negro and White Children: A Psychological Study in the Rural South*. New York: Academic Press, 1968.
Boney, J. D. "Predicting the Academic Achievement of Secondary School Negro Students." *Personnel and Guidance Journal*, 1977, *44*, 700–703.
Campbell, J. T., Crooks, L. A., Mahoney, M. H., and Rock, D. *An Investigation of Sources of Bias in the Prediction of Job Performance: A Six-Year Study*. ETS Report PR-73-37. Princeton, N.J.: Educational Testing Service, 1973.
Chapman, M., and Hill, R. A. (Eds.). *Achievement Motivation: An Analysis of the Literature*. Philadelphia: Research for Better Schools, 1971.
Clark, K. B. *Dark Ghetto: Dilemmas of Social Power*. New York: Harper & Row, 1965.
Cleary, T. A. "Test Bias: Prediction of Grades in Negro and White Students in Integrated Colleges." *Journal of Educational Measurement*, 1968, *5*, 115–124.
Cole, N. S. "Bias in Selection." *Journal of Educational Measurement*, 1973, *10*, 237–255.
Costello, J. "Effects of Pretesting and Examiner Characteristics on Test Performance of Young Disadvantaged Children." *Proceedings of the 78th Annual Convention of the American Psychological Association*, 1970, *5*, 309–310.
Darlington, R. B. "Another Look at 'Culture Fairness'." *Journal of Educational Measurement*, 1971, *8*, 71–82.
Donlon, T. F., and Angoff, W. H. "The Scholastic Aptitude Test." In W. H. Angoff (Ed.), *The College Board Admissions Testing Program*. New York: College Entrance Examination Board, 1971.
Dyer, P. J. "Effects of Test Conditions on Negro-White Differences in Test Scores." Unpublished doctoral dissertation, Columbia University, 1970.
Ebel, R. L. "In Defense of Standardized Testing." Paper presented at the Houghton-Mifflin Annual Measurement Conference, Iowa City, Iowa, March 31, 1976.
Einhorn, H. J., and Bass, A. R. "Methodological Considerations Relevant to Discrimination in Employment Testing." *Psychological Bulletin*, 1971, *75*, 261–269.
Flaugher, R. L. "The Many Definitions of Test Bias." *American Psychologist*, 1978, *33*, 671–679.

Fox, L. H. "Sex Differences in Mathematical Precocity: Bridging the Gap." In D. P. Keating (Ed.), *Intellectual Talent: Research and Development*. Baltimore, Md.: Johns Hopkins University Press, 1976.

Gordon, R. A., and Rudert, E. E. "Bad News Concerning IQ Tests." *Sociology of Education*, 1979, *52*, 174–190.

Gross, A. L., and Su, W. "Defining a 'Fair' or 'Unbiased' Selection Model: A Question of Utilities." *Journal of Applied Psychology*, 1975, *60*, 345–351.

Guilford, J. P. *The Nature of Human Intelligence*. New York: McGraw-Hill, 1967.

Hunter, J. E., and Schmidt, F. L. "A Critical Analysis of the Statistical and Ethical Implications of Various Definitions of 'Test Bias'." *Psychological Bulletin*, 1976, *83*, 1053–1071.

Jackson, R. "The Scholastic Aptitude Test: A Response to Slack and Porter's 'Critical Appraisal'." *Harvard Education Review*, 1980, *50*, 382–391.

James, W. S. "Symposium on the Effects of Coaching and Practice in Intelligence Tests: 11. Coaching for All Recommended." *British Journal of Educational Psychology*, 1953, *23*, 155–162.

Jensen, A. R. *Educability and Group Differences*. New York: Basic Books, 1973.

Jensen, A. R. *Bias in Mental Testing*. New York: Free Press, 1980.

Kennedy, W. A., Van de Riet, V., and White, J. C., Jr. "A Normative Sample of Intelligence and Achievement of Mexico Elementary School Children in the Southeastern United States." *Monographs of the Society for Research on Child Development*, 1963, *28*, no. 6.

Linn, R. L. "Fair Test Use in Selection." *Review of Educational Research*, 1973, *43*, 139–161.

Matarazzo, J. D. *Wechsler's Measurement and Appraisal of Adult Intelligence* (5th ed.). Baltimore, Md.: Williams & Wilkins, 1972.

McGurk, F. C. J. "Race Differences—Twenty Years Later." *Homo*, 1975, 219–239.

McGurk, F. C. J. "Socioeconomic Status and Culturally Weighted Test Scores of Negro Subjects." *Journal of Applied Psychology*, 1953, *37*, 276–277.

Miele, F. "Cultural Bias in the WISC." *Intelligence*, 1979, *3*, 149–164.

Nichols, P. L. "The Effects of Heredity and Environment on Intelligence Test Performance of 4 and 7-Year-Old White and Negro Sibling Pairs." Unpublished doctoral dissertation, University of Minnesota, 1972.

Noble, C. E. "Race, Reality, and Experimental Psychology." *Perspectives in Biology and Medicine*, 1969, *13*, 10–30.

Novick, M. R., and Petersen, N. C. "Toward Equalizing Educational and Employment Opportunity." *Journal of Educational Measurement*, 1976, *13*, 77–88.

Petersen, N. C., and Novick, M. R. "An Evaluation of Some Models for Culture-Fair Selection." *Journal of Educational Measurement*, 1976, *13*, 3–29.

Quay, L. C. "Language, Dialect, Reinforcement, and the Intelligence Test Performance of Negro Children." *Child Development*, 1971, *42*, 5–15.

Quay, L. C. "Negro Dialect and Binet Performance in Severely Disadvantaged Black Four-Year-Olds." *Child Development*, 1972, *43*, 245–250.

Quay, L. C. "Language, Dialect, Age, and Intelligence-Test Performance in Disadvantaged Black Children." *Child Development*, 1974, *45*, 245–250.

Roberts, J. *Intellectual Development of Children by Demographic and Socioeconomic Factors*. DHEW Publication No. 72–1012. Washington, D.C.: U.S. Government Printing Office, 1971.

Rumenik, A. K., Capasso, D. R., and Hendrick, C. "Experimenter Sex Effects in Behavioral Research." *Psychological Bulletin*, 1977, *84*, 852–877.

Sarason, I. G. "The Test Anxiety Scale: Concepts and Research." In C. D. Spielberger and I. G. Sarason (Eds.), *Stress and Anxiety*, Vol. 5. Washington, D.C.: Hemisphere, 1978.

Sattler, J. M. *The Assessment of Children's Intelligence*. Philadelphia: Saunders, 1974.

Scarr, S., and Weinberg, R. A. "IQ Test Performance of Black Children Adopted by White Families." *The American Psychologist*, 1976, *10*, 726–739.

Shockley, W. "Morals, Mathematics, and the Moral Obligation to Diagnose the Origin of Negro IQ Deficits." *Review of Educational Research*, 1971, *41*, 369–377.

Shockley, W. "Dysgenics, Geneticity, Raciology: A Challenge to the Intellectual Responsibility of Educators." *Phi Delta Kappan*, 1972, *53*, 297–307.

Slack, W. V., and Porter, D. "Training, Validity, and the Issue of Aptitude: A Reply to Jackson." *Harvard Educational Review*, 1980a, *50*, 392–401.

Slack, W. V., and Porter, D. "The Scholastic Aptitude Test: A Critical Appraisal." *Harvard Educational Review*, 1980b, *50*, 154–175.

Solkoff, N. "Race of Experimenter as a Variable in Research with Children." *Developmental Psychology*, 1972, *7*, 70–75.

Stanley, J. C. "Further Evidence via the Analysis of Variance that Women Are More Predictable Academically than Men." *Ontario Journal of Educational Research*, 1967, *10*, 49–56.

Stanley, J. C. "Predicting College Success of the Educationally Disadvantaged." *Science*, 1971, *171*, 640–647.

Stanley, J. C., and Porter, A. C. "Correlation of Scholastic Aptitude Test Scores with College Grades for Negroes Versus Whites." *Journal of Educational Measurement*, 1967, *4*, 199–218.

Thorndike, R. L. "Concepts of Culture-Fairness." *Journal of Educational Measurement*, 1971a, *8*, 63–70.

Thorndike, R. L. "Memorandum on the Use of the Lorge-Thorndike Tests in California." Unpublished paper, February 26, 1971b.

Thurstone, L. L. *The Vectors of the Mind*. Chicago: University of Chicago Press, 1935.

Vernon, P. E. *Intelligence and Attainment Tests*. London: University of London Press, 1960.

Yates, A. "Symposium on the Effects of Coaching and Practice in Intelligence Tests: An Analysis of Some Recent Investigations." *British Journal of Educational Psychology*, 1953, *23*, 147–154.

Lloyd Bond is assistant professor of psychology and research associate at the Learning Research and Development Center at the University of Pittsburgh. He received his Ph.D. degree from The Johns Hopkins University in 1976. Dr. Bond has served as a consultant to the American Association for the Advancement of Science, Educational Testing Service, College Board, and National Urban League. He was a Spencer Fellow of the National Academy of Education in 1980. He has published several articles and book reviews on minimum competency testing, aptitude-treatment interaction (ATI), and the measurement of change. His research interests also include statistical theory and multidimensional scaling. He is guest editor for the special issue of the American Psychologist *on tests and testing.*

Biased test items can be identified by expert judgment and by careful statistical analysis.

Identifying Bias in Test Items

Lorrie A. Shepard

Tests are in the public eye because they guard important gates with a promise of objectivity and fairness. Critics of tests assert that apparent differences in test-score performance among ethnic and socioeconomic groups are the result of bias in the tests rather than real differences in ability (Association of Black Psychologists, 1969; Williams, 1970a, 1970b). They contend that there is only a pretense of scientific objectivity whereby tests are used insidiously to perpetuate existing inequities.

The defenders of tests acknowledge specific instances of cultural bias in some tests but do not believe that the use of tests is necessarily or uniformly unfair. Furthermore, they assert that without tests critical decisions of selection and placement would be made by more subjective means, without explicit criteria, and would be far more vulnerable to prejudice (Messick and Anderson, 1970). Advocates of tests are anxious to eliminate the defects in tests without losing their strengths. Since the early 1970s, because of a heightened awareness that tests might be intrinsically biased as well as sometimes misused, new methodologies have been developed to detect bias in tests and test items.

This chapter is focused on item bias procedures. It is a summary of the item bias literature emphasizing the conceptual basis for bias

B. F. Green (Ed.), *New Directions for Testing and Measurement: Issues in Testing—Coaching, Disclosure, and Ethnic Bias*, no. 11. San Francisco: Jossey-Bass, September 1981.

detection methods and the technical issues involved in choosing among methods. The main text of the chapter is divided into two parts dealing with judgmental and statistical methods for identifying biased test questions. A final section is devoted to the reconciliation of judgmental and statistical evidence of bias. From this discussion recommendations are made for practical applications and for further research on the methods themselves.

By way of introduction to the central text, key terms and distinctions are explained. The introductory definitional sections are especially concerned with locating the literature on item bias in the context of the more general topics, test bias, fairness, and the moral use of tests.

Definition of Bias, Validity, and Fairness

Bias in a test is a slant in the way a test measures what it is intended to measure; it is a systematic error that disadvantages the test performance of one group compared to another. In this way bias is distinguished from other types of measurement error—always of concern in test development—because random errors or a constant source of invalidity are at least "fair" to all groups, that is, treat all groups the same. The issue of bias is most often raised regarding the disadvantage of minority group members on white middle-class-oriented tests. The concept of bias and procedures discussed in this chapter could apply as well to the comparison of males versus females, urban versus rural populations, or other groups who bring different cultural experiences to the test.

The concept of bias is best understood in the traditional framework of measurement validity. A test has validity for a particular purpose if it measures what it purports to measure; that is, the inferences and interpretations made from the test scores are sound. Bias may be thought of as differential validity. That is, the meanings of test performance are not the same for members of different groups. Green (1975) used the example of a measure of word knowledge taken as a measure of intelligence. Although the test might accurately reflect individual differences in reasoning ability for affluent whites, it more likely measures vocabulary or opportunity to learn for blacks.

From the earliest exchanges about test bias, there has been a distinction made between internal properties of a test and fairness in how a test was used. Messick and Anderson (1970) noted, for example, that the testing community had not really responded to Williams's charge of inequitable tests, because measurement specialists had not acknowledged that tests could be intrinsically biased but only conceded that they were often misused. These are really two separate issues as Messick and Anderson explain:

> One issue deals with the whole question of whether a test is any good—for particular types of individuals under particular circumstances—as a measure of the characteristics it purports to assess. The other issue deals with the question of test use, beginning with whether or not a test *should* be utilized for a specific purpose. The first question is a scientific one; it may be answered by appraising the test's psychometric properties, especially its construct validity. The second question is an ethical one; it may be answered by evaluating the potential consequences of testing in terms of human values (pp. 80–81).

In the literature on test bias authors occasionally use the terms bias and unfairness interchangeably. When the distinction is needed, however, there has been a consensus to use *bias* to refer to intrinsic features of a test and *fairness* to refer to ethical questions about how the test is used (Green, 1975; Jensen, 1980; Merz, 1974).

By defining bias as invalidity and at the same time saying that bias is an inherent property of a test, psychometricians have contradicted themselves. The formal concept of validity has always depended on the particular *use* of a test. The test standards (APA/AERA/NCME, 1974) and Cronbach's (1971) important chapter on test validation both emphasize that validity is ascribed to the accuracy of test score interpretations; it is not an enduring characteristic of the test for all applications. In this sense, then, *both* bias and fairness are contextual properties; they can only be judged in light of the particular interpretations or conclusions to be drawn from the test. Nevertheless, there is a distinction worth preserving between relatively more technical issues, about the accuracy of what a test measures, and larger issues of fairness in how (or whether) a test should be used.

The parallelism between validity and relatively more technical, "intrinsic" evidence of unbiasedness is further clouded by an expanding definition of validity in the larger measurement literature. In the past, validity has been subdivided into three "types" or means for gathering evidence: content validity, criterion-related validity and construct validity (APA/AERA/NCME, 1974). This division has apparently fostered the misconception that any one type of evidence would be sufficient, that logical validity would be enough for achievement tests and predictive validity enough for college admissions tests. Clearly, however, the soundness of any test depends both on logical demonstrations of relevance and empirical confirmation that indeed the test measures as intended. In the old terminology, then, only the conception of construct validity was sufficiently comprehensive, including requirements for both logical validity and multiple sources of empirical validity. Recently there has been a call for a more unified conceptualization of validity (Cronbach, 1980; Dunnette and Borman, 1979; Guion, 1977, 1978, 1980; Linn, 1980; Messick, 1979; Tenopyr, 1977) and a corresponding application to the evidence for unbiasedness (Berk, forthcoming (a)). Cronbach (1980) not only eschewed the separate, narrow routes to validity but extended the arguments necessary to defend the use of a test to include questions of values. It is not enough to demonstrate, for example, that a selection test is highly correlated with success in law school but we should also consider whether anything essential would be lost by changing the mode of instruction for the benefit of low scorers. The expanded conception of validity is best captured in this quotation: "We might once have identified validation with a single question, What does the instrument measure? That question will not have an objective, universal answer. A yet more judgmental question now takes on equal importance: And why should *that* be measured?" (Cronbach, 1980, p. 107). This larger view of validity is now more congruent with the term "fairness." Referring back to the earlier distinction made by Messick and Anderson, validity has grown to include both scientific and ethical issues. Ellett (1980), for example, demonstrated that fairness—in weighing a good but fallible test for college admissions—can only be addressed by means of moral debate.

A full understanding of what is implied by validity and fairness is necessary to see what item bias methods can and cannot do. These terms are used as points of reference throughout the chapter. Judgmental methods for detecting biased items may well bear on the larger issue, "Should *that* be measured?" The statistical methods, however, only help to resolve questions of invalidity in the old sense, "Is the measurement accurate?" By Cronbach's (1980) more demanding view of validity, then, satisfactory conclusions from these methods will be only one of the "guy wires necessary to support the validity claim." Evidence of unbiasedness in the narrow sense will be necessary but not sufficient to establish the fairness of a test.

Judgmental Methods

Expert judgment is involved at each stage of test development. Logical validity is not accomplished by a separate phase tacked on at the end, rather it is established (or not) by the wisdom and coherence of the reasoning at each step. The phases of test development include specification of the content or construct domain, sampling from the domain, item writing, pilot testing, item review and revision, and assembly of the final test. Since important judgments are involved at each step there could be corresponding checks at every juncture to ensure unbiasedness. More practically, items are usually reviewed for bias late enough in the sequence of test construction to catch errors in any one of several preceding steps. For purposes of this discussion, issues in logically ensuring unbiasedness are subsumed by two major considerations: judgments involved in the initial rationale for specification of the test content domain and judgmental reviews of items.

Constructing the Test Domain. The meaning of a test score depends ultimately on how well the items on the test represent the intended subject matter or implied ability. Establishing logical validity is often characterized as a sampling problem, that is, the accuracy of the inferences made from the test will depend on how well the test content domain is specified and how well the items sampled represent the test content domain. The more ambiguous the definition of the intended domain or the more elusive our grasp of the intended construct, the more potential there is for what is captured in the test to be a distortion of the intended meaning. Although measurement experts now realize that even well specified achievement domains are vulnerable to such distortions, it is generally true that the content universe can be much more clearly explicated for achievement tests than for aptitude or ability measures. Ability tests have greater potential for bias because they aim at more abstract concepts and require greater inferences.

The validity of achievement tests is greatly enhanced by the methods of domain specification developed as part of criterion-referenced testing (see Millman, 1974; Popham, 1978, 1980). These procedures provide for greater detail in mapping the content domain and include item generating rules as part of the domain description. Even so, representing the domain is not reduced merely to a problem of random sampling from the domain. Much still depends on the insightfulness of the particular item writer. Hence, the call for empirical corroboration as well as content validation (Hambleton, 1980b; Linn, 1980; Messick, 1979).

If adequate domain specifications ensure that test content is appropriate, then bias in achievement tests will usually be the result of irrelevant difficulty. There may be problems in how the question is posed or in the format of the item that prevent examinees from answering correctly even though they have mastered the concept. Both item reviews and statistical techniques discussed in later sections are designed to catch such sources of bias. It is not considered to be an instance of bias when a well-constructed achievement test reflects real differences in what groups have been taught. Bias can creep in, however, when differences in opportunity to learn in different subject areas are mixed together, as, for example, when group differences in math achievement are confounded by reading abilities. Reading difficulty on a math test is a source of invalidity for all groups but may differentially affect one group more than another. This is the type of bias best prevented by better test development in the first place, that is, by careful domain specification. Finally, it should be noted that even the best achievement test can lead to biased conclusions if inferences are drawn beyond its purpose. Flaugher (1980) pointed out that achievement tests were most vehemently charged with bias when they were *interpreted* as measures of aptitude, namely, when low scores of minority students were attributed to lack of ability rather than inadequate instruction.

Measures of ability cannot simply be tailored to a well articulated domain. Although there is an enormous body of research on human intelligence and cognitive processes there is not a consensual, concrete definition of what intelligence is, nor, more narrowly, what scholastic aptitude is. Each test author has a basic understanding of the concept and must invent items that will manifest the trait. The process is like reaching blindly into a large bag containing the trait and pulling elements from it without ever seeing the complete contents of the bag. Even with rigorous empirical confirming techniques (that indeed the items are from the right bag) there is the risk that oddities in the sampling from the trait will interact with group differences to the disadvantage of one group. This potential for bias will be especially great when a narrow subset of items, all of one type, are taken to stand for the entire trait.

Measures of learning aptitude usually establish logical validity by creating "reasoning" tasks using content that is either equally unfamiliar to everyone (for example, nonsense syllables or fictional propositions) or very familiar to everyone (for example, elementary arithmetic in a test given to high school seniors). If the measures correlate in expected ways with performances that the ability is expected to predict, the validity claim is strengthened. It is here that more could be done to consider the issues of "fairness" raised by Cronbach's (1980) more demanding view of validity. Consider, for example, the following number series items where the instructions are to identify the next number in the series:

						Answer Choices			
						a	b	c	d
1.	2	4	6	8	___	9	10*	12	16
2.	2	3	5	8	___	9	10	11	12*
3.	7	11	13	17	___	18	19*	20	23

*correct answers.

Would it add or detract from the validity of the test as a measure of reasoning ability to give instructions with similar items until examinees were all familiar with the variety of ways that the numbers could be related? "See the answer to number one is achieved by adding two to each number but number two is harder because you have to find the *pattern* in the numbers that are added." It might be argued that the mental operations involved in inventing and testing new possible solutions are exactly the abilities we are trying to measure; that is, that instruction would reduce the validity of the task as a measure of ability. (Although surely reasoning would still be involved in generalizing the instructional strategies to new problems.) But suppose there are cultural differences in examinees that make one group more likely than another to try completely different strategies when they reach a point in the test where solutions that worked earlier are no longer correct. If there are group differences in test wiseness—in realizing that the rules can change in the middle of the game—then the instruction would make it a fairer test. Such questions should be given greater attention when developing the rationale for an aptitude measure. The issue could also be addressed empirically. Does instruction with test strategies reduce group differences? Is the predictive validity of the instrument enhanced or reduced? For the latter question, of course, we must be clear that the criterion does not have parallel biases requiring test wiseness or inside knowledge about the rules of the game.

In addition to pervasive cultural differences that might influence the examinees' approaches to taking a test, we must also be on the lookout for differences in experience that change the meaning of specific items. Question three in the example was contrived as an example of "irrelevant difficulty" that can create bias in aptitude measures. The solution to question three is easy for the test taker who knows about prime numbers. However, for the examinee who has not learned about prime numbers, deducing the underlying principle would be a far more difficult reasoning problem (further confused by other complex patterns of "skipping odd numbers").

Bias in individual test items is likely to be caught by item reviews or item bias statistical techniques treated in the remainder of the chapter. Pervasive bias in the way a test domain is conceptualized can best be forestalled by asking more searching questions at the outset about "Why should *that* be measured?" Validity at this step is more important than at any other stage in test development.

Item Reviews. In response to charges of bias and because of much greater sensitivity to problems of racism and sexism in our society, all major test publishers have developed formal guidelines for the treatment of minorities, women, handicapped people, and even inhabitants of different geographic regions and urban versus rural communities. These guidelines are intended to prevent bias in how members of different groups are portrayed in test materials; the guidelines are used to train test authors but are also the basis for careful item reviews. Expert reviewers are usually subject matter experts who also represent one of the potentially disadvantaged groups.

The literature on judgmental methods for eliminating test bias is devoted almost entirely to expert reviews for "editorial" or "facial" bias. The concern is with material that might be inappropriate or offensive for members of one group, that is, would appear "on its face" to be biased. The formal procedures followed by six major test publishers are summarized in Berk (forthcoming (b)) by representatives of publishing firms (Green and others, forthcoming). Across all the guidelines, key elements include rules and examples for avoiding stereotyped portrayals and biased language and for representing minorities and women in test materials proportionately to their number in the population. Although formal guidelines for bias reviews deal primarily with the portrayal of members of minorities and other significant groups, in practice these reviews are also intended to detect items with ambiguous meaning for members of particular groups.

A serious limitation of judgmental bias review procedures is that experts are unable to recognize consistently which questions will be relatively more difficult for members of particular groups. In studies by Jensen (1977), Sandoval and Miille (1980), and Plake (1980), judges performed at only a chance level in identifying items that would be relatively more difficult for members of minority groups. For example, Jensen (1976) reported that the frequently cited biased item on the WISC, "What is the thing to do if a fellow (girl) much smaller than yourself starts to fight with you?" had a higher order in difficulty rankings for whites than for blacks, that is, it was relatively easier for blacks. These findings do not eliminate the need for editorial review since it is important to remove objectionable content whether or not it has an effect on test performance. Furthermore, statistical indices of relative difficulty are not sensitive to carry-over effects such as might occur if an offensive item dampened performance on several subsequent items (Shepard, forthcoming). The discouraging results of judgmental bias detection methods have lead, however, to the conclusion that the effects of bias on the meaning of test questions may be too subtle to be easily discerned, hence the need for statistical techniques to uncover unanticipated bias.

The literature on judgmental methods conveys an unfortunate emphasis on cosmetic or editorial concerns rather than on systematic rules for reevaluating the fidelity with which the test construct is represented. It has been presumed that if positive role models were depicted for both males and females, and for members of minority groups that the test would be fair to all groups. The more fundamental concern, that the test measure the same thing for all groups, is presumed to have been dealt with largely by the initial efforts to establish logical validity. In a comprehensive chapter on judgmental methods, Tittle (forthcoming) discussed two categories of procedures: those dealing with stereotyping, positive representation and familiarity and those regarding judgments about opportunity to learn. In the first category extensive detail was given for sensitizing judges regarding defamatory terminology, and so on; only two studies were cited where authors tried to analyze ways in which differences in background could alter the meaning of test questions. Tittle also reviewed classification schemes and taxonomies that are useful in judging the curricular fairness of achievement tests, namely, the match between what is supposed to be taught, what is actually taught, and what is covered on the test. However, these methods are more appropriate for determining whether a test is fair for use in evaluating an educational *program*. The "opportunity to learn" methods do not—at least as far as they are currently developed—attend to the more subtle problem of two *individuals* who have received equal instruction but who may not have an unbiased opportunity to show what they have learned because of differences in their experiences outside of school.

As has been stated previously, judgmental item reviews are expected to catch items with ambiguous meaning for some groups, but very little has been done to structure what judges should look for. A suggested item review form by Hambleton (1980a) is exemplary because it does give attention to familiarity with how questions are asked as well as to potentially offensive material. For each test item, judges are asked to answer "yes" or "no" to the following questions:

1. Is the item free of offensive sexual, cultural, racial, and/or ethnic content?
2. Is the item free of sexual, cultural, racial, and/or ethnic stereotyping?
3. Is the item free of language that could be offensive to a segment of the examinee population?
4. Is the item free from descriptions that could be offensive to a segment of the examinee population?
5. Will the activities or situations described in the item be familiar to all examinees?
6. Will the words in the item have a common meaning to all examinees?
7. Is the item free of difficult vocabulary and/or sentence structure?
8. Will the item format be familiar to all examinees?

The last four questions are crucial but crude. There is virtually no further guidance from the literature about what constitutes bias in each of these instances. Everything depends on the insight of the item reviewer (to detect the shortsightedness of a similarly trusted item writer). Interestingly enough, the first attempts to detail bias categories about distortions in meaning that might be instructive to future reviewers are coming now as part of the effort to try to interpret the results of statistical bias studies. In a forthcoming chapter, Scheuneman dramatically improved the level of discourse by developing a framework for identifying sources of bias peppered with actual examples. Because her analysis is better applied after consideration of statistical indices of bias, it will be considered in the final section of this chapter, in the section on reconciling statistical and judgmental methods.

In summary, judgmental methods are important for ensuring the logical relevance of test items as well as the appearance of fairness. Heretofore, the literature on judgmental methods has been absorbed with stereotypic portrayals and pejorative language. Following these guidelines and instincts, however, judges have consistently failed to identify items that are differentially more difficult for particular groups. It is for this reason that statistical methods were developed to locate instances of differential difficulty. Perhaps then from this research will come better understanding of bias so that in the future distortions of the intended construct can be prevented when the test is first conceived. Ultimately the guidelines for establishing logical validity across groups should be as thorough and thoughtful as current guidelines for eliminating stereotypes.

Statistical Methods

Anomaly and Interaction Definitions of Bias. Several well known statistical methods for detecting biased items are reviewed in the following sections. They are technically different but all follow the same line of reasoning; that is, each method works by locating deviant items, those that do not have the same between-groups pattern as the rest of the items in the test. For example, after controlling for overall differences in group means, items that are unusually difficult for one group are flagged. The shift in item statistics is taken as evidence that a particular item is not functioning the same as other items, perhaps measuring something different for different groups. This has been referred to as the "anomaly" (Shepard, Camilli and Averill, 1980; Shepard, forthcoming) or "interaction" (Jensen, 1974) conception of bias.

Statistical item bias techniques are all internal methods. In one sense this will always be a serious limitation of the methods; it means that they cannot detect pervasive or systematic bias. Just as external methods would be useless with a biased criterion, so internal methods are insensitive to bias that is equally in all the items. Statistical detection techniques work to find the "worst" items in a test. As we shall see, this is just one of the reasons that statistical approaches must be used in conjunction with judgmental methods that ensure the logical validity of the overall conceptualization of the test.

Having acknowledged the caveat, however, it is misleading to consider item bias methods only as weak approximations of external methods. Instead, they address a different question quite well. They check, in a different way, how well and how consistently the test maker has gotten at the intended construct. Their strength is in the availability of multiple items (in a test or subtest) all intended to measure the same thing. Because the elements are analyzed separately it is possible to detect distortions or differential meanings in what was thought to be a homogeneous set of items. Internal methods provide a more direct test of the test makers' efforts to sample from the construct domain.

Differential Item Difficulties. Using a scaling technique devised by Thurstone (1925), Angoff (1972) proposed a bias detection method based on transformed item difficulties. It is one of the most common methods in practice, frequently used, for example, by the Educational Testing Service as a screening device in test development (see Carlton and Marco in Green and others, forthcoming). It is also referred to as the Angoff or delta-plot method. The transformed item difficulty approach identifies items as biased if they are *relatively* more difficult for one group than another.

Item difficulties or p-values (the proportion of examinees getting the item right) are first computed separately for each group. The within-group p-values are then *transformed* to normal deviates by obtaining the z-value corresponding to the (1-p)*th* percentile. The resulting values are called deltas and are usually linearly adjusted to have a mean of 13 and standard deviation of 4. (The statistical purpose for the transformation is to eliminate curvilinearity in the relationship between deltas for the two groups.) A bivariate graph is constructed with delta values for one group along one axis and deltas for the other group along the other axis. The items that are very difficult for members of both groups will appear in the upper right-hand corner of the two-dimensional plot. Those that are easy in both groups will appear in the lower left corner. If the items have the same relative difficulty in both groups they will fall in a narrow ellipse from the lower left- to the upper right-hand corner. Items that are relatively more difficult for members of one group will be seen as sharp departures from the line. In Figure 1, an example given by Raju (in Green and others, forthcoming) shows the effect on final test

Figure 1. Example of Delta Plot Method for Detecting Biased Items from Raju (Green and others, in press) Showing Elimination of Items with Differential Difficulty from Pretest to Standardized Version of the SRA Reading Comprehension Test (Level E).

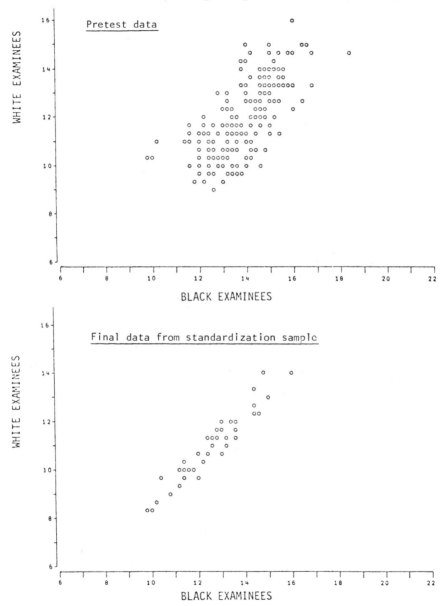

data for the SRA Reading Comprehension test (Level E) of eliminating all pretest items that had large delta discrepancies between blacks and whites.

Although the procedure is conceptually similar to correlational scatter-plots, it is not appropriate to compute a least-squares regression solution since there are no arguments as to why the deviations should be minimized in one direction (that is, one group regressed on the other). Instead, a major axis or principal axis line is fit to the data which minimizes perpendicular deviations. Formulae for obtaining the principal axis and for computing deviations (the bias index) are given in Angoff and Ford (1973). A refinement of the technique, which prevents the influence of discrepant items on the determination of the principal axis, was used in a study by Sinnott (1980). Several variations of the transformed item difficulty method exist and are summarized in Angoff (forthcoming).

The most serious drawback to the delta-plot method is that p-values are contaminated by group differences as well as item difficulty. When there are differences in the means of two groups being considered, highly "discriminating" items will appear to be biased because they will better distinguished between the groups, that is, show larger differences between them. Discrimination in the measurement sense means to accurately differentiate between those who know a concept and those who do not. The problem is best illustrated by the graph in Figure 2. "Item characteristic curves" show the relationship between different levels of achievement (plotted on the abscissa) and the proportion getting the item correct (on the ordinate). Highly discriminating items (like item 1) have steeply rising curves; they can make sharp distinctions within a narrow range on the achievement continuum. Poorly discriminating items are frequently missed by high achieving examinees and answered correctly by low achieving examinees; as a result, the increase in proportion correct is a fairly flat curve (like item 2). If two groups have different mean ability levels and if the item curves cross in the region between the means, as shown in Figure 2, then the more discriminating item will have the largest difference in proportions correct without in any way measuring something different. This fallacy in the transformed item difficulty approach is thoroughly explained in Angoff (forthcoming), Cole (1978), Hunter (1975), and Lord (1977a).

Angoff (forthcoming) discussed a strategy for coping with this serious deficiency in the delta-plot method. To avoid misinterpreting artifactual effects of real ability differences, groups should be matched beforehand on ability, as was done in the Angoff and Ford (1973) study. A highly relevant variable would have to be used for matching but it

Figure 2. Item Characteristic Curves for Two Items
with Different Discriminations

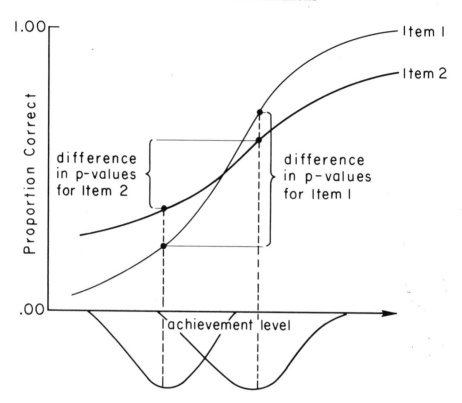

could not be done using the test itself since this would build in circular relationships. This solution is not perfect but may be desirable in situations where the simpler delta-plot procedure is practical. The item-response theory approach considered later is theoretically better but is also much more costly and complex to execute. Angoff (forthcoming) also explained other inadequacies of the transformed item difficulty approach with potential corrections.

Finally, Angoff (forthcoming) considered another important conceptual point in interpreting the results of the delta-plot procedure. In any array of items there is likely to be some variability in delta discrepancies that are not large enough to be considered as signs that the items are measuring something different. We would observe these fluctuations, for example, if we constructed random groups and plotted delta values for them. Angoff suggested that a more legitimate way to establish what the base rate should be in interpreting deviations would be to observe the usual variance in delta differences obtained from widely different samples—for whom a test is considered appropriate—from within the *same* sex or ethnic group. The example he used was to compare whites in the Northeast with rural whites in the South.

Item Response Theory Methods. Item response (or latent trait) theory provides a more elegant model than classical test theory for describing the characteristics of an item as a function of an underlying ability or trait dimension. A mathematical function can be derived for each item on a test, the item characteristic curve, which reflects the probability of getting the item right for examinees at every ability level. Theoretical item characteristic curves were shown in Figure 2 as part of the discussion of the delta-plot method. From that example it can be seen how crude classical p-values are in reflecting how the item functions at different locations on the ability continuum. The reader who is unfamiliar with item response theory may wish to consult Lord (1980) and Lord and Novick (1968), or the special issue of the *Journal of Educational Measurement* on latent trait models (1977).

The most important feature of item response theory is that it provides sample invariant (or relatively sample invariant) estimates of item parameters. This means that the estimates of item difficulty are not confounded by the achievement level of the particular group studied, hence it is much less likely that artifactual instances of bias will be present. Bejar (1980), Lord (1977a, 1977b, 1980), Petersen (1977), and Wright (1977) have all concluded that item response theory is the most theoretically sound method for detecting biased items.

The item characteristic curve or function is defined by three parameters: a variable that is proportional to the slope of the curve at the inflection point (the a parameter); the location of the inflection point along the ability dimension (the b parameter); and the lower asymptote (the c parameter). The a, b, and c parameters are better understood conceptually as the item discrimination, difficulty, and guessing values, respectively. Using this three-parameter model, an item is considered to be biased if the item characteristic curves for two groups are not the same. Because the parameter estimates are not dependent on the particular group sampled, the same curves should be obtained even for groups with very different average abilities.

There is also a one-parameter latent trait model referred to as the Rasch model (Rasch, 1966). By some simplifying assumptions—that there is no guessing on the test and that all items are equally discriminating—the Rasch model uses logistic functions to describe item characteristic curves that only vary in difficulty parameters. Using the Rasch model, bias is defined either as group differences in difficulties or lack of model fit for one group.

Currently, in the measurement literature there is considerable debate over the relative merits of the one- and three-parameter latent trait models for many measurement applications. Very simplistically, the difference of opinion is between those who want a model that will fit the data and those who would prefer to tailor the data to fit a model. Because the three-parameter model has more parameters it will almost always fit real data better. Wright (1977) and others would argue, however, that the measurement characteristics that the Rasch model assumes are highly desirable and, therefore, items should not be used in a test (entirely apart from the question of bias) unless they satisfy these conditions. Regardless of which model should be emulated in the ideal, it is true that the one-parameter model will yield spurious results if it is applied to data that do not meet its assumptions. Although the Rasch model may well produce adequate estimates of examinee abilities—at lower cost and with smaller sample sizes—it has generally been found not to be as good as the three-parameter model in applications where the individual item parameters are of interest, as is the case with item bias (see Divgi, 1981a, 1981b; Ironson, forthcoming; Reckase, 1981). Moreover, the Rasch difficulty index of bias is virtually identical to the Angoff procedure (see Shepard, Camilli, and Averill, 1980).

A chapter by Ironson (forthcoming) is a good reference for issues involved in using latent trait bias methods as well as the chi-square approaches considered in the next section. Two computer programs are available for obtaining item parameters with the three-parameter model, LOGIST (Wood and Lord, 1976; Wood, Wingersky, and Lord, 1976) and ANCILLES (Urry, 1978). A minimum of 40 items and 1,000 examinees are recommended for adequate estimation. After item parameters are estimated separately in two groups, they must be equated to the same scale; then several operationalizations exist for quantifying the difference in item characteristic curves for two groups. These bias indices include simple differences between each of the parameters and both signed and unsigned measures of the areas between the curves (see Rudner, 1977; Ironson and Subkoviak, 1979; and Shephard, Camilli, and Averill, 1980). Signs are attached to the bias indices to indicate which group is disadvantaged by the difference in item characteristic curves, that is, which group has the lower probability of a correct response for the same ability level. When one curve is always to the left of the other across the entire ability continuum, the signed and unsigned area measures have the same meaning. However, if the curves cross, one group has the advantage in one region and the other is ahead in the other region. In these cases the signed area index will have a low value because the biases are compensating. The unsigned area (or absolute value) measure of bias will show the total amount of incongruence between the curves regardless of direction. Lord (1980) has demonstrated the usefulness of yet another index, a significance test that compares the differences in *b* values for two groups taking into account the standard error of the differences for that comparison.

The three-parameter method for detecting biased items is preferred theoretically and has been found to be the best at detecting simulated bias in actual studies (Merz and Grossen, 1979; Rudner, Getson, and Knight, 1980). This method is costly, however, because of the requirements for large sample sizes and elaborate computer programs. Because these methods are very new and research is still being done on the details of implementing the procedures, it is not known how errors in the procedures could lead to errors in the detection of bias. Especially it is not clear how serious the instability of the item parameters (especially *a* and *c* parameters) or problems at the equating stage are in obscuring bias or in creating artifactual bias. Here, then, is another reason that statistical results from even the most sophisticated method must be mediated by logical analysis of item content.

Chi-square Methods. Chi-square methods (Camilli, 1979; Green and Draper, 1972; Scheuneman, 1975, 1979) for detecting bias are rough approximations of the latent trait models. They follow the same definition of unbiasedness, that is, individuals with the same ability should have the same probability of success on the item regardless of group membership. To establish comparable ability groups, the total test score range is divided into discrete intervals, usually five. Scheuneman (1979) has likened these intervals to crude stairsteps replacing the smooth item characteristic curves. Within each score interval, examinees from different ethnic groups or sexes are expected to have the same probability of getting the item correct.

To compute the chi-square for an item, expected values are established for each interval assuming the probability of answering correctly to be uncorrelated with group membership. Then, the observed proportions are compared with the expected proportions using a chi-square (or modified chi-square) goodness-of-fit statistic. Large deviations from expected frequencies, summed across intervals (in the form, $\frac{(O-E)^2}{E}$) will result in large χ^2 values signifying a biased item. Scheuneman's (1975, 1979) method is the most well known. Computational examples and a discussion of the types of items found to be biased in the *Metropolitan Readiness Test* are given in Scheuneman (1979).

As discussed by Camilli (1979), there is a logical flaw in the Scheuneman chi-square procedure because it is based on only proportions correct. Chi-square statistics computed from proportions correct

(p) across ability strata for different groups will lead to different results than if the χ^2 were calculated using proportions incorrect (q). The full chi-square, using both proportions correct and incorrect, is therefore preferable and has the advantage of known sampling distributions for the purposes of significance testing (see the critique by Baker, 1981). Scheuneman (1981) preferred the modified procedure on practical grounds because with very easy items it is difficult to construct intervals with adequate cell sizes for the full procedure; oddly though, bias will more likely be found in easy items with the full procedure. It can also be argued that the need for a significance test (and hence known distributional characteristics) is secondary to the need for a bias index (see Shepard, Camilli, and Averill, 1980). Final conclusions regarding bias should be made on logical grounds and should be more influenced by deviance from other items addressing the same construct than by the power of the statistical test.

The more important rebuttal from Scheuneman (1981) and an overriding consideration with both chi-square procedures is this: These methods are approximate. They should be regarded as practical alternatives in situations where small sample sizes or limitations in computer facilities make it impossible to use the three-parameter latent trait method. Even more serious limitations to the chi-square methods are that the matching by intervals may be so crude that regression artifacts will create the appearance of bias, and that matching on total score builds in a systematic bias in the detection technique. (At least these are usually compensating effects.) Ultimately, however, even with statistical improvements such as matched groups, the answer should be to treat bias indices as tools that can only be used in conjunction with a thorough understanding of the test and what it is intended to measure. A significant χ^2 value (or its absence) should not lead automatically to the conclusion that an item is biased (or not).

Reconciling Judgmental and Statistical Evidence of Bias

A surprising finding in attempts to logically review items for bias was that expert judges, usually representing minority groups, were unable to predict successfully which items were likely to be harder for particular groups (Jensen, 1977; Plake, 1980; Sandoval and Miille, 1980). This has been, in fact, an important impetus for developing statistical techniques to detect bias in test questions. Perhaps an even more unsettling finding, however, has been that the results of statistical studies are often uninterpretable, that is, many items identified as biased do not have any obvious signs of bias even when scrutinized with the wisdom of hindsight. As Scheuneman (forthcoming) recalls, many researchers in this area had "naively assumed that a review of such items would readily reveal the source of the apparent bias, that the problem could then be easily corrected with suitable modifications or by dropping the item from the test or item pool, and that a 'debiased' instrument would result." To be sure, a number of researchers have found consistent and explainable instances of bias (Draba, 1977; Ironson and Subkoviak, 1979; Rudner, 1978; Scheuneman, 1976, 1979). But, the number of uninterpretable occurrences of biased items is disconcertingly large and leaves the test maker with a dilemma. Has the statistical indicator uncovered a real instance of bias, revealing a blind spot in the conceptualization of the construct, or is the large bias index a statistical artifact, that is, not a valid sign of bias? In this concluding section some techniques and further topics for research are proposed which may help reduce the "dross rate" from statistical methods. In addition, an important work by Scheuneman (forthcoming) is summarized that should be useful in guiding logical analysis of empirical findings.

The validity evidence for bias detection methods themselves is mixed. The several empirical studies comparing bias methods find that the three prominent methods, delta-plot, chi-square, and three-parameter latent trait, are moderately correlated with each other. Since each has a different source of artifactual error, this suggests that they are "converging" on true instances of bias. These three methods are also reasonably good at detecting simulated bias (see Rudner, Getson and Knight, 1980). Consistent with expectations, Ironson and Subkoviak (1979) found much less bias in white-white comparison groups using these methods than in white-black comparisons. Also, Shepard, Camilli, and Averill (1980) found patterns of correlation and amount of bias that were predictable from the type of test and particular minority group abilities. Although sometimes the particular items identified are not interpretable, often they are as when Scheuneman (1979) found a consistent problem with negatively worded items with black kindergarten and first grade children.

Nevertheless, as stated in Shepard, Camilli, and Averill (1980): "Although the congruence among methods is sufficient to hearten a measurement theorist, the practitioner is more likely to be struck by the serious method effects observable in the results. The method one chooses will make a difference in the number of items found to be biased and in the particular set of items labeled biased" (p. 74). Even the theoretically preferred method, the three-parameter latent trait method only correlates on the order of 0.8 with generated bias (Merz and Grossen, 1979; Rudner, Getson and Knight, 1980). This was true even though in both studies the bias had been generated using a three-parameter latent trait paradigm. One must conclude then that either random errors or problems in implementing the equating phase prevented better "recovery" of the bias that had been built in.

The following suggestions are made for ways to reduce artifactual and hence uninterpretable instances of bias:

1. As explained previously, Angoff has suggested a priori matching of groups on a relevant variable as a way of coping with the confounding of true group differences when using the transformed item difficulty method. This strategy has appeal as well for the chi-square method which is vulnerable to regression effects when the groups being compared are not equal on overall means. Even the three-parameter method, which is theoretically sample invariant, may have difficulties when differences between groups are large. (In vertical equating studies, for example, the three-parameter method was superior to equatings using the Rasch model but demonstrated some instability (Kolen, 1981).) It would be worth checking whether such matching reduces the amount of bias indicated or changes the particular items identified.

2. Cross-validation studies would be an effective means to determine what test items are uniformly biased in comparisons between two groups. Although this suggestion would escalate the requirements for large sample sizes even more than the already great demands for implementing the three-parameter method, it should be considered at least for research on the nature of bias even if it could not be done in most practical applications. If, for example, a test were being examined for bias between blacks and whites, large samples of each group could be randomly split in half. Since estimation errors and peculiarities in the sample should not be the same in both comparisons, the items identified as biased in both data sets are more likely truly biased and should be more interpretable. It should be noted, of course, that unless the data sets are very large initially, say several thousand in each ethnic group, greater estimation errors may be introduced for the three-parameter method by cutting the sample in half. Moreover, it is unlikely that suggestions one and two could be implemented concurrently since matching also causes reduction in sample size (by losing cases at each end) when there are mean differences.

3. The two-step procedures followed by Lord (1977a, 1980) and Sinnott (1980) have wider applicability. For each bias detection method it is wise to try to minimize the influence of the most biased items on intermediate steps in the statistical computations. Therefore, whether one is determining the major axis for the delta-plot method or for equating b parameters in the latent trait method or estimating person ability values, it is better to implement the given procedure in two stages. In the

first step items should be tentatively identified as biased and removed from more refined and less contaminated determinations of bias in the second step.

4. Finally, Angoff's (forthcoming) recommendation for establishing a base rate for interpreting bias is crucial. Although he proposed it for implementing the transformed item difficulty method, it is equally applicable to other methods. To gain an understanding of how much spurious "bias" may be created by sampling fluctuations and vagaries of the methods, it is important to try them with very different groups for whom the test is equally appropriate such as two groups of whites from different regions but matched on ability.

The preceding suggestions are aimed at tinkering with technical features of statistical bias methods to try to improve their validity in identifying real, rather than spurious occasions of bias. Especially, the methods themselves and some of these additional strategies attend to the problem of true group differences that should not be mistaken for bias. But in the end, this issue must be addressed logically as well as technically.

Scheuneman (forthcoming) provides a framework for considering and interpreting statistical evidence of bias. In essence the arguments of this chapter come full circle. The logical connections established initially between test items and the construct domain must be reexamined in light of the new evidence of differential group performance. As suggested by Scheuneman the overarching question to be deliberated is whether the "bias" index signals a distortion in meaning between groups, hence real bias, or a true difference in knowledge that legitimately should be assessed in keeping with the purpose of the test. The conclusion of bias and the decision to throw items out of the test will depend on what abilities the test was intended to represent. As several authors have noted (Angoff, forthcoming; Green and others, forthcoming) the term *bias index* is a misnomer; the various methods actually identify "deviant" or "discrepant" items. The labels of item bias methods have misled people to think that differential group performance is automatically an indication of bias; it is not. Scheuneman (forthcoming) and Angoff (forthcoming) use examples of certain types of math problems having to do with square roots and percentages that are more difficult for blacks than whites relative to other items, yet are valid measures of math knowledge not yet acquired. It will be a matter of judgment to decide for the particular purpose of the test whether group discrepancies imply bias.

The references just cited are important reading for anyone attempting to do this type of screening for bias. They contain numerous examples of types of items flagged as deviant and the kind of reasoning that leads to the conclusion of bias or not. Examples are essential in learning about these issues since they virtually defy concrete stipulative definitions.

Scheuneman (forthcoming) provides more detail than any other author about categories of bias encountered and how bias reviews should be organized to find these types of errors. In the near future there should be much more formal work of this kind. Scheuneman includes usual examples of items where the format of a question is biased or where particular vocabulary words have a special meaning in black dialect. But she also has found less obvious examples, such as differential familiarity with what was being asked that was manifested as a positional effect. This and other examples, like the differential effects of speededness, lead to the general admonition that bias should always be interpreted in the context of other items. It will often take a large pool of items before subtle trends emerge.

In summary, logical analyses following statistical analyses of bias should recapitulate the initial test development stages of construct definition and rationale for item selection. Deviant item statistics may signal a change in the meaning of items across groups or may only reflect true performance differences between groups. A thoughtful reconsideration is needed of what each item is measuring. What are the plausible distortions in meaning or sources of irrelevant difficulty? There are not cut-and-dried statistical procedures for resolving questions of bias. Judgment and scientific reasoning are needed to determine whether a trait is measured fairly. Moreover, as Cronbach (1980) has urged in his more encompassing view of validity, moral reasoning will be needed to substantiate that it is fair that *that* trait is measured.

References

American Psychological Association, American Educational Research Association, and National Council on Measurement in Education. *Standards for Educational and Psychological Tests* (rev. ed.). Washington, D.C.: American Psychological Association, 1974.

Angoff, W. H. "A Technique for the Investigation of Cultural Differences." Paper presented at the meeting of the American Psychological Association, Honolulu, September 1972.

Angoff, W. H. "Use of Difficulty and Discrimination Indices for Detecting Item Bias." In R. A. Berk (Ed.), *Handbook of Methods for Detecting Test Bias*. Baltimore, Md.: Johns Hopkins University Press, forthcoming.

Angoff, W. H., and Ford, S. F. "Item-Race Interaction on a Test of Scholastic Aptitude." *Journal of Educational Measurement*, 1973, *10*, 95–105.

Association of Black Psychologists, Position Statement Adopted at a Meeting of the Association in Washington, D.C., September 1969.

Bejar, I. I. "Biased Assessment of Program Impact Due to Psychometric Artifacts," *Psychological Bulletin*, 1980, *87*, in press.

Berk, R. A. "Introduction." In R. A. Berk (Ed.), *Handbook of Methods for Detecting Test Bias.* Baltimore, Md.: Johns Hopkins University Press, forthcoming (a).

Berk, R. A. (Ed.). *Handbook of Methods for Detecting Test Bias.* Baltimore, Md.: Johns Hopkins University Press, forthcoming (b).

Camilli, G. "A Critique of the Chi-Square Method for Assessing Item Bias," Unpublished paper, Laboratory of Educational Research, University of Colorado, Boulder, 1979.

Cole, N. S. "Approaches to Examining Bias in Achievement Test Items." Paper presented at the national meeting of the American Personnel and Guidance Association, Washington, D.C., March 1978.

Cronbach, L. J. "Test Validation." In R. L. Thorndike (Ed.), *Educational Measurement* (2nd ed.). Washington, D.C.: American Council on Education, 1971.

Cronbach, L. J. "Validity on Parole: How Can We Go Straight?" W. B. Schrader (Ed.), *New Directions for Testing and Measurement: Measuring Achievement: Progress Over a Decade.* San Francisco: Jossey-Bass, 1980.

Divgi, D. R. "Does the Rasch Model Really Work? Not If You Look Closely." Paper presented at the annual meeting of the National Council on Measurement in Education, Los Angeles, April 1981a.

Divgi, D. R. "Potential Pitfalls in Applications of Item Response Theory." Paper accompanying discussant comments at the annual meeting of the National Council on Measurement in Education, Los Angeles, April 1981b.

Draba, R. E. "the Identification and Interpretation of Item Bias." *Research Memorandum No. 26.* Statistical Laboratory, Department of Education, University of Chicago, 1977.

Dunnette, M. D., and Borman, W. C. "Personnel Selection and Classification Systems." In M. R. Rosenzweig and L. W. Porter (Eds.), *Annual Review of Psychology* Vol. 30. Palo Alto, Calif.: Annual Reviews, 1979.

Ellett, F. S. "Fairness and the Predictors." Paper presented at the annual meeting of the American Educational Research Association, Boston, 1980.

Flaugher, R. L. "The many definitions of test bias." *American Psychologist,* 1978, *33,* 671–679.

Green, D. R. "What Does It Mean to Say a Test Is Biased?" *Education and Urban Society,* 1975, *8,* 33–52.

Green, D. R., Coffman, W. E., Lenke, J. M., Raju, N. S., Handrick, F. A., Loyd, B. H., Carlton, S. T., and Marco, G. L. "Methods Used by Test Publishers to Debias Standardized Tests." In R. A. Berk (ed.), *Handbook of Methods for Detecting Test Bias.* Baltimore, Md.: The Johns Hopkins University Press, forthcoming.

Green, D. R., and Draper, J. F. "Exploratory Studies of Bias in Achievement Tests." Paper presented at the annual meeting of the American Psychological Association, Honolulu, September 1972.

Guion, R. M. "Content Validity, the Source of My Discontent." *Applied Psychological Measurement,* 1977, *1,* 1–10.

Guion, R. M. "'Content Validity' in Moderation." *Personnel Psychology,* 1978, *31,* 205–213.

Guion, R. M. "On Trinitarian Doctrines of Validity." *Professional Psychology,* in press.

Hambleton, R. K. "Review Methods for Criterion-Referenced Test Items." Paper presented at the annual meeting of the American Educational Research Association, Boston, April 1980a.

Hambleton, R. K. "Test Score Validity and Standard Setting Methods." In R. A. Berk (Ed.), *Criterion-Referenced Measurement: The State of the Art.* Baltimore, Md.: Johns Hopkins University Press, 1980b.

Hunter, J. E. "A Critical Analysis of the Use of Item Means and Item-Test Correlations to Determine the Presence or Absence of Content Bias in Achievement Test Items." Paper presented at the National Institute of Education Conference on Test Bias. Maryland, December 1975.

Ironson, G. H., and Subkoviak, M. "A Comparison of Several Methods of Assessing Item Bias." *Journal of Educational Measurement,* 1979, *16,* 209–225.

Ironson, G. H. "Use of Chi-Square and Latent Trait Approaches for Detecting Item Bias." In R. A. Berk (Ed.), *Handbook of Methods for Detecting Test Bias.* Baltimore, Md.: Johns Hopkins University Press, forthcoming.

Jensen, A. R. "How Biased Are Culture-Loaded Tests?" *Genetic Psychology Monographs,* 1974, *90,* 185–244.

Jensen, A. R. "Test Bias and Construct Validity." *Phi Delta Kappan,* 1976, *58,* 340–346.

Jensen, A. R. "An Examination of Cultural Bias in the Wonderlic Personnel Test." *Intelligence,* 1977, *1,* 51–64.

Jensen, A. R. *Bias in Mental Testing.* New York: Free Press, 1980.

Journal of Educational Measurement, Special issue on applications of latent trait models, 1977, *14,* 73–196.

Kolen, M. J. "Comparison of Traditional and Item Response Theory Methods for Equating Tests." *Journal of Educational Measurement,* 1981, *18,* 1–11.

Linn, R. L. "Issues of Validity for Criterion-Referenced Measures." *Applied Psychological Measurement,* 1980, *4,* 547–561.

Lord, F. M. "A Study of Item Bias Using Item Characteristic Curve Theory." In Y. H. Poortinga (Ed.), *Basic Problems in Cross-Cultural Psychology.* Amsterdam: Swets and Zeitlinger, 1977a.

Lord, F. M. "Practical Applications of Item Characteristic Curve Theory." *Journal of Educational Measurement,* 1977, *14,* 117–138.

Lord, F. N. *Applications of Item Response Theory to Practical Testing Problems.* Hillsdale, N.J.: Erlbaum, 1980.

Lord, F. M., and Novick, M. R. *Statistical Theories of Mental Test Scores.* Reading, Mass.: Addison-Wesley, 1968.

Merz, W. R. "A Biased Test May Be Fair, But What Does That Really Mean?" Paper presented at the meeting of the California Educational Research Association, San Francisco, 1974.

Merz, W. R. "Test Fairness and Test Bias: A Review of Procedures." In M. J. Wargo and D. R. Green (Eds.), *Achievement Testing of Disadvantaged and Minority Students for Educational Program Evaluation.* Monterey, Calif.: CTB/McGraw-Hill, 1978.

Merz, W. R., and Grossen, N. E. "An Empirical Investigation of Six Methods for Examining Test Item Bias." Report submitted to the National Institute of Education, Grant NIE-6-78-0067, California State University, Sacramento, California, 1979.

Messick, S. "Test Validity and the Ethics of Assessment." Paper presented at the annual meeting of the American Psychological Association, New York, September 1979.

Messick, S., and Anderson, S. "Educational Testing, Individual Development, and Social Responsibility." *Counseling Psychologist,* 1970, *2,* 80–88.

Millman, J. "Criterion-Referenced Measurement." In W. J. Popham (Ed.), *Evaluation in Education: Current Applications.* Berkeley, Calif.: McCutchan, 1974.

Petersen, N. S. "Bias in the Selection Rule: Bias in the Test." Paper presented at the Third International Symposium on Educational Testing, University of Leyden, The Netherlands, June 1977.

Plake, B. S. "A Comparison of a Statistical and Subjective Procedure to Ascertain Item Validity: One Step in the Test Validation Process." *Educational and Psychological Measurement*, 1980, *40*, 397–404.

Popham, J. S. *Criterion-Referenced Measurement*. Englewood Cliffs, N.J.: Prentice Hall, 1978.

Popham, W. J. "Domain Specification Strategies." In R. A. Berk (Ed.) *Criterion-Referenced Measurement: The State of the Art*. Baltimore, Md.: Johns Hopkins University Press, 1980.

Rasch, G. "An Individualistic Approach to Item Analysis." In P. F. Hazarsfeld and N. W. Henry (Eds.), *Readings in Mathematical Social Science*. Chicago: Science Research Associates, 1966.

Reckase, M. D. "The Validity of Latent Trait Models Through the Analysis of Fit and Invariance." Paper presented at the annual meeting of the American Educational Research Association, Los Angeles, April 1981.

Rentz, R. R., and Bashaw, W. L. *Equating reading tests with the Rasch model*. Athens, Ga.: Educational Resource Laboratory, 1975.

Reynolds, C. R. "The Problem of Bias in Psychological Assessment." In C. R. Reynolds and T. B. Gutkin (Eds.), *The Handbook of School Psychology*. New York: Wiley, 1981.

Rudner, L. M. "An Approach to Biased Item Identification Using Latent Trait Measurement Theory." Paper presented at the annual meeting of the American Educational Research Association, New York, 1977.

Rudner, L. M. "Using Standardized Tests with the Hearing Impaired: The Problem of Item Bias." *The Volta Review*, 1978, *80*, 31–40.

Rudner, L. M. "Biased Item Detection Techniques." *Journal of Educational Statistics*, 1980, *5*, in press.

Rudner, L. M., Getson, P. R., and Knight, D. L. "A Monte Carlo Comparison of Seven Biased Item Detection Techniques." *Journal of Educational Measurement*, 1980, *17*, 1–10.

Rudner, L. M., and Convey, J. J. "An Evaluation of Select Approaches for Biased Item Identification." Paper presented at the annual meeting of the American Educational Research Association, Toronto, March 1978.

Sandoval, J., and Miille, M. P. W. "Accuracy Judgments of WISC-R Item Difficulty for Minority Groups." *Journal of Consulting and Clinical Psychology*, 1980, *48*, 249–253.

Scheuneman, J. "A New Method of Assessing Bias in Test Items." Paper presented at the annual meeting of the American Educational Research Association, Washington, April 1975.

Scheuneman, J. "Validating a Procedure for Assessing Bias in Test Items in the Absence of an Outside Criterion." Paper presented at the meeting of the American Educational Research Association, San Francisco, April 1976.

Scheuneman, J. "A Method of Assessing Bias in Test Items." *Journal of Educational Measurement*, 1979, *16*, 143–152.

Scheuneman, J. D. "A Posteriori Analyses of Biased Items." In R. A. Berk (Ed.), *Handbook of Methods for Detecting Test Bias*. Baltimore, Md.: Johns Hopkins University Press, forthcoming.

Shepard, L. A. "Definitions of Bias." In R. A. Berk (Ed.), *Handbook of Methods for Detecting Test Bias*. Baltimore, Md.: Johns Hopkins University Press, forthcoming.

Shepard, L., Camilli, G., and Averill, M. "Comparison of Six Procedures for Detecting Test Item Bias Using Both Internal and External Ability Criteria." Paper presented at the annual meeting of the National Council on Measurement in Education, Boston, April 1980.

Sinnott, L. A. "Differences in Item Performance Across Groups." Princeton, N. J.: Educational Testing Service. Report for the Graduate Management Admission Council. Report in preparation, 1980.

Tenopyr, M. L. "Content-Construct Confusion." *Personnel Psychology*, 1977, *30*, 47–54.

Thurstone, L. L. "A Method of Scaling Educational and Psychological Tests." *Journal of Educational Psychology*, 1925, *16*, 263–278.

Tittle, C. K. "Judgmental Methods in Test Development." In R. A. Berk (Ed.), *Handbook of Methods for Detecting Test Bias*. Baltimore, Md.: Johns Hopkins University Press, forthcoming.

Urry, V. *ANCILLES: Item Parameter Estimation Program with Ogive and Logistic Three-Parameter Options*. Washington, D.C.: U.S. Civil Service Commission, Personnel Research and Development Center, 1978.

Williams, R. L. "Black Pride, Academic Relevance, and Individual Achievement." *Counseling Psychologist*, 1970a, *2*, 18–22.

Williams, R. L. "Danger: Testing Dehumanizing Black Children." *Clinical Child Psychology Newsletter*, 1970b, *9*, 5–6.

Wood, R. L., and Lord, F. M. *A User's Guide to LOGIST*. Research Memorandum. Princeton, N.J.: Educational Testing Service, 1976.

Wood, R. L., Wingersky, M. S., and Lord, F. M. *LOGIST: A Computer Program for Estimating Examinee Ability and Item Characteristic Curve Parameters*. Research Memorandum. Princeton, N.J.: Educational Testing Service, 1976.

Wright, B. D. "Solving Measurement Problems with the Rasch Model." *Journal of Educational Measurement*, 1977, *14*, 97–116.

Lorrie A. Shepard is associate professor and chair of the Research and Evaluation Methodology Division in the School of Education, University of Colorado, Boulder. From 1978–1980 she was the editor of the Journal of Educational Measurement; *currently she is the vice-president and president-elect of the National Council on Measurement in Education.*

*Test disclosure legislation ruined a perfectly good method of
score equating. How is this important to test takers and
what alternatives are open to test makers?*

Equating Tests in an Era of Test Disclosure

Gary L. Marco

The LaValle Act in New York State, which was signed into law in July
1979 and became effective in January 1980, requires that examinees be
given the opportunity to see the test questions used in obtaining their
scores on postsecondary school admission tests. This and other provisions of the LaValle Act were enacted only after considerable debate
about the advantages and disadvantages of test disclosure. Opponents
of the legislation argued not only that test disclosure would preclude
the reuse of test forms and thus drive costs up, but that for many of
the major aptitude tests changes would have to be made in the procedures
for ensuring that scores are approximately equivalent from one edition, or form, of a test to another.

This process of adjusting scores on a test form to make them
approximately equivalent to scores on another form is called "equating."
Equating is necessary in instances where scores from different test forms
are used interchangeably to make decisions about test takers, as in the
case of major admissions tests such as the ACT Assessment, the
Graduate Management Admission Test, the Graduate Record Examina-

B. F. Green (Ed.), *New Directions for Testing and Measurement: Issues in
Testing—Coaching, Disclosure, and Ethnic Bias*, no. 11. San Francisco:
Jossey-Bass, September 1981.

tions Aptitude Test, the Law School Admission Test, and the Scholastic Aptitude Test. New forms of these tests are produced each year and administered at regular national administrations.

"Equating" is a technical word that is not easy for the public to understand. This chapter helps the general reader to understand the equating issues associated with test disclosure. It also helps the testing practitioner to recognize situations in which equating is necessary and to understand how to accomplish various kinds of equating. The chapter is not intended to be a primer on equating methods, but it does provide a rationale for equating and describe some common equating methods. The mathematical detail associated with equating methods is held to a minimum. Interested readers can obtain more complete information about the methods from the references given at the end of the chapter.

Why Is Equating Needed?

It is no surprise that the public has difficulty understanding the equating problems posed by testing legislation. Even classroom teachers and measurement specialists do not usually recognize the need for equating. One reason for this is that books on educational and psychological testing, even advanced textbooks, used in undergraduate and graduate courses rarely refer to equating, although the related topics of standardization and norming are almost always discussed. (Reference books like Thorndike, 1971, do give the topic adequate treatment.) It is not clear why equating has not been given much emphasis in the testing literature, but it probably relates to the fact that the kinds of standardized tests used by teachers, guidance counselors, and others have only a limited number of forms. It is only for those testing programs that frequently offer new forms of their tests that there is a clear need for equating.

The lack of general information about equating in books on educational and psychological testing explains to some extent why the need for equating often goes unrecognized. But even those who are trained in graduate schools to be measurement specialists often overlook the importance of equating. Measurement specialists learn about test theory, the technical aspects of test development, reliability, and validity. Many, however, leave graduate school with the notion that producing forms that yield approximately equivalent scores is strictly a test development problem, that test development experts can select test questions in such a way that resulting differences among test forms are small and unimportant.

Test developers have a number of methods at their disposal for helping them develop test forms that are parallel in some sense. Test specifications usually exist in the form of a table of content specifications, which gives the topics and skills to be measured. In addition, statistical specifications are often used in testing programs that try out test questions (items) before they are used in final forms. Statistical specifications for a test are usually given in terms of item difficulty indices, such as the percentages of examinees responding correctly to the items. The mean and standard deviation of the item difficulties and the frequency distribution of item difficulties are two common ways in which statistical specifications are expressed. The mean item discrimination index (for example, the biserial correlation of the item score, where 1 = right and 0 = wrong, with the score on the test to which the item belongs) may also be included in the statistical specifications. More elaborate statistical specifications are sometimes provided in the form of a two-way frequency distribution of item difficulties and item discrimination indices.

Gulliksen (1950), in writing about matched random subtests, suggested that approximately parallel test forms could be assembled by the following steps: (1) plot the item difficulties and item discrimination indices, (2) identify items that cluster together on the plot, and (3) assign one of the items in each cluster to each form by a random process. Of course, item content would have to be considered in assigning items so that the test forms would be approximately parallel in terms of their content as well as their statistics. Even without item statistics, items could be matched on the basis of their item content and format (that is, type of item: analogies, antonyms, and so on) and assigned randomly to one of the forms.

Such methods help the test developer to control the variation in test questions from test form to test form. But how successful are these methods? How similar are the scores that result from forms assembled to both content and statistical specifications? Table 1 shows the form-to-form variation in the scores of the GRE Aptitude Test and the Scholastic Aptitude Test (SAT). This table gives the range of scaled scores corresponding to particular raw scores for several forms of each test. The raw score on either test is computed by counting the number of right answers and subtracting a fraction of the number of wrong answers—one third in the case of four-response multiple-choice questions and one fourth in the case of five-response questions. Questions omitted by the examinee do not count toward the scoring. For each test form, by means of equating methods like those discussed later, a rule is derived for transforming, or converting, the raw scores to the scale for the test. (The GRE Aptitude Test scale extends from 200 to 900; the SAT scale, from 200 to 800.)

The score ranges in the table indicate the variation present after test forms have been assembled to fairly rigorous statistical specifica-

Table 1. Scaled Score Ranges Corresponding to Particular Raw Scores for the GRE Aptitude Test and the Scholastic Aptitude Test (SAT)

Raw Score	GRE Aptitude Test[a]			SAT[b]	
	Verbal (80 questions)	Quantitative (55 questions)	Analytical (70 questions)	Verbal (85 questions)	Mathematical (60 questions)
85				800	
80	850–870			740–770	
75	810–850			710–730	
70	770–810		770–800	670–700	
65	730–760		730–780	640–660	
60	680–720		680–740	600–620	800
55	640–680	830–840	640–690	570–590	740–770
50	600–630	770–780	600–650	530–550	690–720
45	560–590	710–730	560–610	500–520	650–670
40	520–540	650–670	520–560	460–480	600–620
35	480–500	600–610	470–420	430–450	560–580
30	440–450	540–550	430–480	390–410	520–540
25	400–410	480–490	390–430	350–370	470–490
20	350–370	420–440	350–390	320–340	430–450
15	310–330	370–380	310–350	280–310	390–410
10	270–290	310–320	270–310	250–270	350–370
5	230–250	250–260	220–270	210–240	300–330
0	200–210	200	200–230	200	260–290

[a]The GRE-Verbal and GRE-Analytical score ranges are based on five GRE Aptitude Tests administered between January 1980 and February 1981; the GRE-Quantitative score ranges are based on four GRE Aptitude Tests administered between April 1980 and February 1981 (*Source:* the Graduate Record Examinations Program, 1980a, 1980b, 1980c, and 1980d).

[b]The SAT score ranges are based on all editions of the SAT given between 1974 and 1977 (*Source:* The Admissions Testing Program, 1978).

tions. Note, for example, that a raw score of 70 on GRE-V converts to a scaled score of 770 in one case and to a scaled score of 810 in another. If the test forms had not been equated, a raw score of 70 would have been treated as if it represented the same ability level across forms. Yet it may be seen from the table that on one form (a slightly easier one) a raw score of 75 converted to a scaled score of 810, whereas on a more difficult form a raw score of 70 converted to this same scaled score. The seriousness of this form-to-form variation, of course, depends upon the use of the scores. For admissions use, even a small amount of variation could be important. Without equating, the college admissions officer would certainly have difficulty convincing the examinee who took a more difficult test form that the examinee was treated fairly in the admissions process. This is why equating is so important to test takers—it ensures, as nearly as possible, that the reported test scores are fair expressions of underlying knowledge, abilities, or skills regardless of the test form actually taken.

Some Common Equating Methods

Even if we are convinced that equating is necessary for controlling form-to-form differences in test difficulty, it is not always clear what methods to use. Here only a few of the possible methods that might be used are discussed. But, first, it is necessary to understand what equating means.

What Equating Is Not. Those who have read an elementary textbook in educational and psychological testing, once they are aware of equating procedures, may have difficulty distinguishing between the process of standardizing scores and the process of equating scores. The results of both processes can be given in the form of a table showing converted, or scaled scores, corresponding to raw scores. Almost every textbook in educational and psychological testing covers the topics of standard scores. Among the standard scores usually discussed are the z-score, with a mean of 0 and a standard deviation of 1, and the T-score, with a mean of 50 and a standard deviation of 10. Some textbooks even discuss normalized standard scores such as stanines, which have a mean of 5 and a standard deviation of approximately 2.

So it is not too surprising to find that students of testing who hear about equating for the first time may think they are already familiar with the topic. But standardizing and equating are not the same. Standardizing refers to the establishment of the scale on which test scores are to be reported. Equating refers to the perpetuation of the scale when new forms of a test are introduced. Tests of different content areas may all be standardized to the same scale. For example, SAT-Verbal and SAT-Mathematical scores are reported on the College Board scale, which was established by setting the mean of examinees who took SAT-Verbal in April 1941 equal to 500 and the standard deviation equal to 100. (See Angoff, 1971a, for detailed information about the scaling process.) Tests of different content areas, however, cannot be equated. Equating can be accomplished only if the tests measure the same underlying knowledge, skills, or abilities. Such tests are assumed to yield scores that are related perfectly except for measurement error. Equating is the process of adjusting the scores on one of the test forms to make them correspond in numerical value to the scores on the other form for a particular population of examinees. (The nature of this correspondence is clarified later.) There is no statistical adjustment that will make a verbal test, say, measure the same skills or abilities as a mathematical test and make them yield scores that are perfectly related except for measurement error.

The distinction between scaling and equating may be clear from a consideration of the Fahrenheit thermometer. When Gabriel Fahrenheit, a German physicist, developed the use of mercury in thermometry, he established a temperature scale that registers the freezing point of water as 32 and the boiling point of water as 212 under standard atmospheric pressure. Once the scale was established, it was perpetuated by calibrating the scale gradients of new thermometers to the established scale. The process of calibration is similar conceptually to the process of equating (although statistical procedures differ). In order for the results of the process to have meaning, new thermometers must measure the same underlying physical phenomenon—temperature. Similarly, if scores from different test forms are to have the same meaning, the forms must measure the same characteristic(s) or factor(s).

In practice, whether tests measure the same underlying factors is a matter of judgment—usually based on a consideration of the test content. However, recent developments on the analysis of covariance structure (Jöreskog, 1971) now make it possible to apply statistical criteria as well.

The Many Definitions of Equating. Equating has been defined in a number of ways over the years. Early definitions of equating (see, for example, Gulliksen, 1950 and Lord, 1950) stressed the necessity of matching the score distributions of examinees taking the tests to be equated. Although not a requirement of the definition, it was understood that the tests to be equated were supposed to measure the same characteristics. Later definitions made explicit the notion that the underlying trait was being measured by the tests to be equated and that scores were equivalent when they corresponded to the same level on the underlying trait. Recently Lord (1977, 1980) went further by tying together the ideas of equity and equating. He stated that it should be a matter of indifference to the examinees which forms of a test they take and proceeded to formalize this requirement in mathematical terms. Of the definitions that follow, Definitions 1 and 2 represent the earlier thinking, and Definitions 3 through 6, the later thinking. Definition 6 states formally the requirement of equity.

Associated with each definition is a set of statistical procedures that yield results consistent with the definition. Here the meaning of the definitions is explicated without any particular emphasis on the statistical procedures associated with them. The definitions are expressed in terms of test scores, for tests scores, not tests, are equated. All of the definitions apply to a defined population of individuals. Theoretically, equating is invariant across populations, but in practice the results will depend at least somewhat on the characteristics of the individuals making up the population.

Definition 1: Scores from Test X and Test Y are equated if $M_{y'} = M_x$ and $SD_{y'} = SD_x$ for a particular population of individuals. Here M stands for mean, SD stands for standard deviation, and y' refers to the score that results from applying a transformation (rule) to y to make it equivalent to x. In this case a linear transformation suffices: $y' = (SD_x/SD_y) y + M_x - (SD_x/SD_y) M_y$. In general, M_y will not equal M_x and SD_y will not equal SD_x because of differences in the difficulties of the test questions in the test forms. The linear transformation adjusts M_y to equal M_x and SD_y to equal SD_x and is referred to as setting means and standard deviations equal. Those familiar with standard scores will recognize this as placing the z-scores on Test Y onto the Test X scale. There is nothing in this definition that requires individual y' scores to be approximately the same as corresponding x scores; only the means and standard deviations must be equal in the population of interest. Nor does the definition qua definition require Test X and Test Y to measure the same underlying knowledge, abilities, or skills.

Definition 2: Scores from Test X and Test Y are equated if y' and x have the same percentile rank in the distributions of Test X and Test Y scores for a particular population of individuals. The transformation that satisfies this definition is given by the equipercentile procedure. The percentile rank of each y is computed and then the corresponding percentile in the distribution of scores on Test X is determined. In practice, the distributions of x and y scores are treated as continuous rather than discrete, and percentile ranks and percentiles are computed by linear interpolation. The distributions may be smoothed before computations are performed. The equipercentile transformation changes the shape (skewness, kurtosis, and so on) of the distribution of Test Y scores to match the shape of the distribution of Test X scores. A linear transformation does not change the shape of the distribution, but may approximate the equipercentile transformation if the shapes of the x and y distributions are similar to begin with. In general, the equipercentile transformation will result in a curvilinear raw-score-to-scaled-score relationship. Here again particular y' scores do not have to approximate corresponding x scores, and the definition does not require Test X and Test Y to measure the same knowledge, abilities, or skills. In fact, as in the case of Definition 1, the correlation between x and y could be negligible and the definition might still be satisfied.

Definition 3: Scores from Test X and Test Y are equated if $M_{y'} = M_x$ for a subpopulation of individuals who have the same underlying knowledge, ability, or skill level; that is, $M_{y'|a}$ (read "mean of y' given a") $= M_{x|a}$ for all a, where a refers to ability level. A curvilinear transformation is usually required to satisfy this definition, but linear procedures may provide useful approximations. The equipercentile transformation may or may not yield results that are consistent with the definition. More complex procedures, such as those associated with item response theory (Lord, 1980, Chapter 13), are usually required. These procedures provide estimates of underlying ability levels. Definition 3 is the only one given thus far that requires Test X and Test Y to measure the same factors. The statistical procedures that yield results that satisfy Definition 3 are based on this assumption. This definition does not say anything about how precise the measurements have to be. Thus, tests producing scores with different reliabilities can be equated according to Definition 3.

Definition 4: Scores from Test X and Test Y are equated if $M_{y'} = M_x$ for every subpopulation of individuals who have the same underlying knowledge, ability, or skill level; that is $M_{y'|a} = M_{x|a}$, and the standard errors of measurement for y' and x are equal for the total population of individuals. This definition adds to Definition 3 the constraint that Tests X and Y must on the average measure with equal precision. In other words, scores on the two tests must have the same reliability. Test X and Test Y must consist of approximately the same number of questions in order for this definition to be satisfied.

Definition 5: Scores from Test X and Test Y are equated if $M_{y'} = M_x$ and $SD_{y'} = SD_x$ for every subpopulation of individuals who have the same underlying knowledge, ability, or skill level; that is, $M_{y'|a} = M_{x|a}$ and $SD_{y'|a} = SD_{x|a}$ for all a. This definition is even more difficult to satisfy than Definition 4, since not only do the overall standard errors of measurement have to be equal but also the standard errors of measurement at every ability level. Practically speaking, this definition is almost impossible to satisfy. Only when test questions are administered by computer and individuals answer enough items to ensure a specific amount of precision will tests come close to meeting the requirements of this definition.

Definition 6: Scores from Test X and Test Y are equated if the frequency distributions of y' and x are the same for a subpopulation of individuals who have the same underlying knowledge, ability, or skill level. Definition 6 is more restrictive than Definition 5 in that the shapes of the conditional distributions of y'|a (as well as $M_{y'|a}$ and $SD_{y'|a}$) must match those for the conditional distribution of x|a. Lord (1980) has shown that this definition is satisfied only if the test questions in Test Y are functionally equivalent to the test questions in Test X or if the two tests yield perfectly reliable scores, in which case y' = x. According to Definition 6 equating cannot be accomplished unless it is impossible or unnecessary! Although this definition is practically impossible to satisfy, strictly speaking it is not a matter of indifference to the examinees whether they take Test X or Test Y unless the requirements of the definition are met.

Fortunately, test scores that are equated by procedures that do not satisfy Definition 6 can be used in practice. But, the decision maker has to take into account the fact that an examinee might earn different scores on different test forms.

An equating method is an empirical procedure for determining a transformation to be applied to scores on a test form to make them equivalent to scores on another test form. Because an equating method is an empirical procedure, it involves a design for data collection and statistical procedures for determining the transformation. Angoff (1971b) covered both aspects in the six equating designs he described. Here the two aspects are treated separately because some statistical procedures can be used with more than one data-collection design. The controversy over equating during the hearings associated with test disclosure legislation arose primarily over data-collection designs, for one of the designs used by a number of major aptitude testing programs could no longer be used if test forms had to be disclosed.

The six definitions given in the previous section were stated as if population data existed on both Test X and Test Y, that is, as if everyone in the population took Test X and Test Y. In actual practice, of course, data are often incomplete. Several of the data collection designs and statistical procedures deal with this situation.

Data-Collection Designs. Table 2 depicts five commonly used designs for collecting equating data. Three basic designs are represented in the table: the single-group design (Design I), the equivalent-groups design (Designs II and III), and the anchor-test design (Designs IV and V).

Design I: One group—both tests administered. Design I is the simplest of the designs and requires only that a single group take both forms of a test, referred to here as "old" form and "new" form. The forms are administered one after the other, preferably on the same day or on two consecutive days. It is important that only a short time elapse between the two testings, so that intervening experiences do not affect the scores. The order in which the tests are administered is not considered important in this design. This means that such factors as learning, practice, and fatigue are assumed to have little effect on the test scores.

Design II: Two random groups—both tests administered to both groups in counterbalanced order. Design II is a modification of Design I in that the single group is divided into two random groups. One group takes the old form first; the other group takes the new form first. If the tests have the same timing, they can be administered in the same room. An easy way to do this is to package the test booklets sequentially so that every other booklet is an old or new form. (This packaging procedure is sometimes called "spiraling.") Then when the booklets are distributed, they are spread evenly among the examinees. The procedure does not result in random samples, but the groups are essentially random if enough examinees (more than 500, say) are tested. Counterbalancing the order of administration ensures that any learning, practice, and

Table 2. Data Collection Designs for Score Equating[a]

Design	Group(s)	Type of Sample	Old Form	New Form	Anchor Test(s)
I	Group 1		D	D	
II	Group 1	Random	D_1	D_2	
	Group 2	Random	D_2	D_1	
III	Group 1	Random	D		
	Group 2	Random		D	
IV	Group 1	Random	D		D
	Group 2	Random		D	D
V	Group 1	Nonrandom	D		D
	Group 2	Nonrandom		D	D

[a]"D" in the table stands for data and indicates that data are collected on the group (in the form of item responses on a test). A blank in the table indicates that data are not collected. A subscript attached to the D indicates the order in which the tests are administered and is given only where order of administration is an essential aspect of the design.

fatigue affect both forms, so that no bias is created in favor of one form.

Design III: Two random groups—one test administered to each group. This design, one of the equivalent-groups designs, requires the administration of the old form to one of the random groups and the new form to the other. If the timings of the tests are the same, the tests can be administered in the same room using the spiraling procedure described previously. It is essential that the two groups be as similar as possible on the knowledge, abilities, or skills being measured, so that the test scores on one form are not too high or too low simply because the group taking the form was more or less able.

This data collection design has been used for the Graduate Management Admissions Test, the Law School Admission Test, and the GRE Aptitude Test. One or two old forms are administered with one or two new forms at a particular test administration. The forms are spiraled so that with three forms, for example, every third examinee takes a given form. Because the forms are administered to large groups, the resulting groups are essentially random for all practical purposes.

Design IV: Two random groups—one test and an anchor test administered to each group. For particular samples this design is superior to Design III in that anchor-test information is available on both random groups. The anchor test may be internal or external. An internal anchor test consists of items spaced throughout the old or new test forms and counted in the test scores; an external anchor test is a physically separate section whose items are not counted in the score for the old or new form. Ideally, the anchor test would be composed of questions like those in the old and new forms. The higher the correlation between scores on the anchor test and scores on the old or new form, the more useful the data are. With random groups, even anchor tests that do not measure the same factors as the old and new forms can provide useful information. It is important, however, that anchor-test data be collected at approximately the same time as the old or new form data. The anchor test should also be administered in the same order to both groups. (For example, if the anchor test is given after the old form, it should also be given after the new form.) Of course, more than one anchor test could be used if time permitted.

The reason that Design IV is superior to Design III is that the old and new form scores can be adjusted to reflect any differences that exist between the random groups on the anchor test. Suppose the group that took the old form had higher scores on the average on the anchor test than the group that took the new form. Then, by appropriate statistical procedures, the old form mean could be lowered or the new form mean raised to the levels that would have been attained had the groups performed equally well on the anchor test. In Design III no adjustments in the scores are possible; random differences, however small, must be tolerated because there is no way of assessing their size. (Random differences associated with Design III can be minimized by using large sample sizes.)

Design V: Two nonrandom groups—one test and an anchor test administered to each group. The data-collection requirements of this design are the same as those for Design IV. However, nonrandom rather than random groups are used. Nonrandom is used here to refer to naturally occurring groups, such as those who happen to take the test at a particular administration. In this design it is important that the anchor test be as similar as possible in content and difficulty to the old and new forms. No statistical procedures can provide completely appropriate adjustments when naturally occurring groups are used, but adjustments based on an anchor test that is parallel to the old and new forms are much more satisfactory than those based on nonparallel anchor tests. A commonly used anchor test is a set of representative items from the old form that are embedded in the new form.

The anchor test scores provide common reference points for equating tests administered to naturally occurring groups, just as the freezing point and boiling point of water provide common reference points for calibrating Fahrenheit and Centigrade thermometers. It is not sufficient to adjust the scores so that all score distributions have the same mean and standard deviation, because the populations of test takers might be different. It is known, for example, that the people who choose to take the GRE Aptitude Test in June are less able on the average than the group taking the test in December.

Design V is the data-collection design used for the SAT. The SAT and its companion test, the Test of Standard Written English, are administered in six separately timed thirty-minute sections. One of the sections consists of questions that are not used in determining the re-ported scores. The content of this section varies—it may contain new, untried questions or it may contain equating items that were adminis-tered with a previous SAT. Several variable sections, including SAT-Verbal and SAT-Mathematical anchor tests, are spiraled with each new form of the SAT. The anchor tests provide the links necessary to equate SAT-Verbal and SAT-Mathematical. More detail regarding the SAT design may be found in Angoff (1971a).

The Impact of Test Disclosure on Data-Collection Designs. Test dis-closure legislation as represented by the LaValle Act in New York State requires that examinees be given the opportunity to see the test ques-tions that contributed to determining their score. Disclosure of old test forms limits the use of designs requiring the administration of both old and new forms (Designs I, II, III, and IV) because of what examinees and others might learn from reviewing questions on the old form. Test disclosure also limits the use of designs requiring internal anchor tests, which are composed of questions from previously administered forms. A review of old questions would cause scores to be higher on the old form than they would otherwise have been. Equating based on these data would result in converted scores on the new form that were too high, since in the equating process scores on the new form are adjusted to conform to scores on the old form.

If samples could be found that had not been exposed to the old forms, they could be used to provide equating data through special equating administrations. The forms for later use in the testing program would be administered along with one or more old forms. There is no guarantee that the equating results based on data collected at special administrations would be satisfactory, for the sample would not neces-sarily represent the test-taking population and, more than that, would not necessarily feel motivated to perform well on the test.

Rather than conducting special equating administrations, testing programs would more likely use an alternative data collection design. Some restructuring of the tests would probably be required, however, to accommodate an alternative design. Design V, used by the SAT, would be one possible alternative, as long as equating items did not have to be disclosed. The LaValle Act protects from disclosure equating items that are not used to obtain reported scores. This does mean, as previously mentioned, that internal anchor tests cannot be used.

Statistical Procedures for Equating. An equating method involves statistical procedures for determining the equating transformation as well as a design for data collection. Statistical procedures that can be used with the various designs presented here have been reviewed by Angoff (1971b). Here only a general overview is given.

When both old and new forms are administered to the same individuals (as in Designs I and II), setting sample means and standard deviations equal and equipercentile equating are the two most commonly used statistical procedures. In the case of Design II, adjustments can be made for "practice" effects (see Lord, 1950 or Angoff, 1971b). Other approaches using item data rather than score data are also possible. When data on both tests are not available on the same group of examinees, the problem is to estimate how the total group would have performed on both tests. Anchor-test information helps in making such estimates by use of regression analysis or other statistical procedures. Once estimates are available, equating procedures appropriate for the total group can be used.

It is important to recognize that equating procedures are similar but different from traditional statistical methods. Those familiar with correlation and regression may on first blush be inclined to equate scores by predicting scores on the old form from scores on the new form. But in equating there is no dependent variable; it is in some sense arbitrary that a particular form was developed and administered before another. A fundamental requirement of equating is that the same results obtain regardless of which form is selected as the old form. Regression methods violate this requirement in that there are two regression lines, not one; and, unless the correlation between scores on the two tests is unity, they result in different transformations for relating scores on one form to scores on the other. Regression methods are used in equating when anchor-test information is available, but not for relating scores on the old and new forms.

Readers interested in conventional formulas used in equating are referred to Lord (1950) and Angoff (1971b). Lord and Angoff also provided formulas for computing sampling errors associated with various types of equating. Recently, Petersen and others (1980) provided comparative data on a large number of statistical procedures appropriate for anchor-test equating.

Equating Options Under Test Disclosure

Because of the test disclosure required by the LaValle Act in New York State and the threat of test disclosure in other states, testing companies have attempted to identify equating methods that might be used in this situation. Three equating methods, which permit equating without requiring the administration of a disclosed form, seem promising. These are anchor-test equating, section pre-equating, and item-response-theory (IRT) equating.

Anchor-Test Equating. The anchor-test method has already been discussed in connection with Designs IV and V. Anchor-test equating can be used as long as equating sections do not have to be disclosed. Only external anchor tests, however, are protected under the LaValle Act. Internal anchor tests must be disclosed because the questions contribute to the reported scores.

Anchor-test equating can be used if (1) a separately timed section can be administered with the operational test (a "nonoperational" section), (2) a miniature version of the test can be developed, and (3) the anchor test is similar to at least one of the other sections of the test in content and timing. The second requirement is not so easy to satisfy as it might seem. If a test consists of many different types of questions, it may be difficult to represent all of them on a short test. Reading passages pose a particular problem in that, because a number of questions accompany each passage, it may be impossible to administer a variety of reading passages in a short test. The third requirement is essential for disguising the anchor test to ensure that examinees try on the questions that do not count toward their scores.

Section Pre-Equating. Section pre-equating and IRT equating both permit equating to take place prior to the time a form is actually administered intact. Section pre-equating requires the administration of a new form of a test, two parts at a time, to random samples at a given test administration. For a four-part test the data collection design can be depicted as follows:

	Old Form	New Form			
		Part 1	Part 2	Part 3	Part 4
Group 1	D	D	D		
Group 2	D	D		D	
Group 3	D	D			D
Group 4	D		D	D	
Group 5	D		D		D
Group 6	D			D	D

(As in Table 2, "D" indicates that data are collected.) This design uses two nonoperational sections. (Under certain conditions, it is possible to use only a single nonoperational section.) Spiraling provides a means to ensure that essentially random groups take parts of the new form. Statistically, the part-test data are used to estimate how all six groups would perform on all four parts of the new form. The estimates are used to relate the new form to the old form, which is taken by every examinee. Statistical procedures that are appropriate for section pre-equating are described in Rubin and Thayer (1978). More detail regarding section pre-equating in general can be found in Holland and Wightman (1980).

The main advantage of this procedure over the anchor-test method, besides those associated with pre-equating, is that essentially random groups are used for equating. Its main advantage over IRT equating is that it is appropriate for equating a test that measures several underlying abilities or skills. (Strictly speaking, IRT equating is appropriate only for tests that measure a single underlying ability or skill.) Its primary disadvantages are that many nonoperational sections have to be used for data collection and that curvilinear equating would be difficult.

Item-Response Theory (IRT) Equating. IRT equating holds some promise for the programs affected by test disclosure in that it can utilize item-response data obtained at earlier, pretest administrations and thus avoid the use of old forms or anchor tests. IRT (also referred to as "latent trait theory" and "item-characteristic curve theory") is a modern replacement for classical test theory. In IRT responses to each test item are related to the underlying continuum of ability (a generic term for what the test measures) by means of an item response curve. The curve indicates the probability of answering the item correctly as a function of ability level. The curve rises from essentially chance performance for examinees of extremely low ability, indicated by the "c parameter," to perfect performance for examinees of extremely high ability. The IRT index of item difficulty, which in classical test theory is the percentage of examinees who answer the item correctly or some function of this percentage, is the ability level at which the probability of a correct answer is halfway between c and 1.00. It is referred to as the "b parameter." The IRT counterpart of the classical item discrimination index, the item-total biserial or point-biserial correlation, is the "a parameter." The parameter is proportional to the slope of the curve at b, the ability level at which the curve is steepest. When a general mathematical form has been specified for the item response curves and the distribution of ability has been determined, the three IRT parameters for each item can be estimated, provided of course that sufficient data exist. Simpler mathematical models (such as the Rasch model), which fix some of the parameters at specific values, have been explored and are useful in some practical situations.

Lord has been instrumental in developing IRT to the point that it can be used to solve practical testing problems. His recent work (Lord, 1980) gives many examples of IRT applications. One chapter is devoted entirely to score equating. The Summer 1977 issue of the *Journal of Educational Measurement* was devoted entirely to applications of latent trait models and contains many good introductory articles. In this issue Marco (1977) and Lord (1977) gave some examples of IRT equating, and Hambleton and Cook (1977) provided a useful introduction to IRT. Two large-scale studies (Rentz and Bashaw, 1975; Marco and others, 1980), designed to compare IRT equating with conventional equating, provide evidence of the usefulness of IRT equating.

IRT equating requires that all of the item-parameter estimates be expressed on the same numerical scale. This can be accomplished by administering some items that have already been calibrated with the new pretests. Once IRT item-parameters estimates are available on a common scale for a sufficiently large item pool, new tests can be assembled from these items. The item-parameter estimates can then be used to determine for any selected level of ability the raw score that would be expected on the new form and the corresponding scaled score. It is this direct relationship between item statistics and total test score that makes IRT so useful in equating.

IRT equating can be used if the following conditions are met: (1) the test consists of items having one correct answer (applications to graded response items are still in the experimental stage); (2) the test is unspeeded or only slightly speeded; (3) the test measures essentially one underlying ability or skill; (4) the item-response curves follow the logistic or some other well-defined mathematical model; (5) item responses are independent of one another for persons at the same level of ability; (6) the test contains enough items to obtain a good estimate of the ability or skill being measured (a minimum of 25, although this is subject to study); and (7) item-parameter estimates are stable across different samples of people and different samples of items. The behavior of IRT equating when these conditions are not met needs to be studied. IRT equating might be possible even when a test measures several abilities or skills. If enough items were administered to adequately measure these abilities or skills and if the items could be categorized as to which abilities or skills they measure, then IRT equating could be applied to each category separately and the results used to equate the total test score. The validity of this kind of equating is open to question; further study is needed before the procedure can be used operationally.

The primary advantage of IRT equating over anchor-test equating, besides those advantages associated with pre-equating, is that anchor tests are not needed, thus saving assembly costs and freeing up the nonoperational section to be used for other purposes. Its main advantage over section pre-equating is that it is unnecessary to use the nonoperational section to administer sections of a future form, thus allowing its use for other purposes and limiting the exposure of the questions in the future form. Another advantage is that equating can be accomplished without readministering the test when a test form is revised to include new items. A disadvantage of IRT equating is that expensive and complex item parameter estimation procedures are frequently required.

If random-group equating must be abandoned because of test disclosure, then anchor-test equating, section pre-equating, and IRT equating appear to be reasonable alternatives. However, some problems must be solved and the feasibility of the approaches studied before any is adopted for operational use. Significant restructuring of a test might be necessary to accommodate any of these equating methods.

References

Admissions Testing Program. *Taking the SAT.* New York: College Entrance Examination Board, 1978.

Angoff, W. H. (Ed.). *The College Board Admissions Testing Program: A Technical Report on Research and Development Activities Relating to the Scholastic Aptitude Test.* New York: College Entrance Examination Board, 1971a.

Angoff, W. H. "Scales, Norms, and Equivalent Scores." In R. L. Thorndike (Ed.), *Educational Measurement* (2nd ed.). Washington, D.C.: American Council on Education, 1971b.

Graduate Record Examinations Program. *Aptitude Tests Administered on January 12, April 26, and April 28, 1980.* Princeton, N.J.: Educational Testing Service, 1980a.

Graduate Record Examinations Program. *Aptitude Test, Edition GR81–1.* Princeton, N.J.: Educational Testing Service, 1980b.

Graduate Record Examinations Program. *Aptitude Test, Edition GR81–2.* Princeton, N.J.: Educational Testing Service, 1980c.

Graduate Record Examinations Program. *Aptitude Test, Edition GR81–3.* Princeton, N.J.: Educational Testing Service, 1980d.

Gulliksen, H. *Theory of Mental Tests.* New York: Wiley, 1950.

Hambleton, R. K., and Cook, L. L. "Latent Trait Models and Their Use in the Analysis of Educational Test Data." *Journal of Educational Measurement,* 1977, *14,* 75–96.

Holland, P. W., and Wightman, L. "Section Pre-equating: A Preliminary Investigation." Paper presented at the ETS Research Statistics Conference on Test Equating, Educational Testing Service, Princeton, N.J., April 2–3, 1980.

Jöreskog, K. G. "Statistical Analysis of Sets of Congeneric Tests." *Psychometrika,* 1971, *36,* 109–133.

Lord, F. M. *Notes on Comparable Scales for Test Scores* (RB–50–48). Princeton, N.J.: Educational Testing Service, 1950.

Lord, F. M. "Practical Applications of Item Characteristic Curve Theory." *Journal of Educational Measurement,* 1977, *14,* 117–138.

Lord, F. M. *Applications of Item Response Theory to Practical Testing Problems.* Hillsdale, N.J.: Erlbaum, 1980.

Marco, G. L. "Item Characteristic Curve Solutions to Three Intractable Testing Curvilinear Score Equating Models." In David J. Weiss (Ed.), *Proceedings of the 1979 Computerized Adaptive Testing Conference.* Computerized Adaptive Testing Laboratory, Department of Psychology, University of Minnesota, September 1980.

Petersen, N. S., Marco, G. L., and Stewart, E. E. "A Test of the Adequacy of Linear Score Equating Models." Paper presented at the ETS Research Statistics Conference on Test Equating, Educational Testing Service, Princeton, N.J., April 2–3, 1980.

Rentz, R. R., and Bashaw, W. L. *Equating Reading Tests with the Rasch Model* (2 vols.). Educational Research Laboratory, College of Education, University of Georgia, September 1975.

Rubin, D. B., and Thayer, D. "Relating Tests Given to Different Samples." *Psychometrika*, 1978, *43*, 3–10.

Thorndike, R. L. (Ed.). *Educational Measurement* (2nd ed.) Washington, D.C.: American Council on Education, 1971.

Gary L. Marco is director of statistical analysis, College Board Programs Division, at Educational Testing Service. A member of the ETS staff since 1964, he has had considerable practical experience in equating tests. In 1979–80 he served as a member of the Advance Program Planning Development Project team, responsible for designing alternative approaches for ETS tesing programs in an era of test disclosure.

Index